16

PULP KITCHEN

The Cookbook

VICKI CHELF

SQUAREONE
PUBLISHERS

COVER DESIGNER: Jeannie Tudor
EDITOR: Michael Weatherhead
TYPESETTER: Gary A. Rosenberg

Square One Publishers
115 Herricks Road • Garden City Park, NY 11040
(516) 535-2010 ● (877) 900-BOOK • www.squareonepublishers.com

Library of Congress Cataloging-in-Publication Data

Names: Chelf, Vicki Rae, author.
Title: Pulp kitchen / Vicki Chelf.
Description: Garden City Park, NY : Square One Publishers, [2016]
Identifiers: LCCN 2015047154 | ISBN 9780757003967 (pbk.) | ISBN 9780757053962
  (e-book)
Subjects: LCSH: Cooking (Vegetables)—By-products. | Cooking
  (Fruit)—By-products. | Food additives. | Plant fibers. | High-fiber
  diet—Recipes. | LCGFT: Cookbooks.
Classification: LCC TX801 .C4335 2016 | DDC 641.5/63—dc23 LC record available at
http://lccn.loc.gov/2015047154

Printed in the United States of America

10   9   8   7   6   5   4   3   2   1

Contents

Acknowledgments

I would first like to thank Rudy Shur, my publisher and friend. Rudy has believed in me for a long time. In fact, it was he who had the idea to write a book about juicing pulp over twenty years ago! I would also like to thank my editor, Michael Weatherhead, for sharing his brilliance with words.

There are a few individuals who have consistently volunteered to eat the results of my experiments, for better or worse, including my husband, John Lambie; Tommy "The Ace" Ducette; and my ex, Jean Renoux. I can always count on them to eat heartily so I can move on to the next recipe. Thanks.

Photographer John Revisky deserves a big thank you for his cover photograph, as does Ana Molinari, who worked her magic with the wig and make-up. Another thank you goes out to graphic designer Jeannie Tudor at Square One, who pulled it all together visually. I would also like to express my gratitude to Shri Shri Ravi Shankar and the teachers at the Art of Living program, who help me to function at a high level.

I would like to thank Vitamix for creating such a wonderful tool. I have few regrets in life, except that I waited so long to get a Vitamix. Last but certainly not least, I would like to thank all my vegan and vegetarian friends out there, who care enough about animals and the planet to walk the talk.

Prologue

What can be done with pulp? Quite a bit, actually. It can be added to breads, cookies, muffins, cereals, veggie burgers, loaves, pâtés, pancakes, porridges, pies, salads, soups, and all sorts of other wonderful dishes. In this book you will find dozens of kitchen-tested recipes that incorporate juicing pulp.

But is there any nutritional value in the pulp of produce that has been run through a juicer? Pulp is certainly a good source of fiber, but what else does it offer? Research shows that pulp has nutritional value, proving that this byproduct is worth saving. It can contain minerals and antioxidants that actually enrich meals when added to recipes.

I know how busy we all are. If anyone is going to use pulp in recipes, doing so better be easy. In light of this fact, Chapter 1 includes a chart that details how much produce is needed to create specific amounts of pulp, and also discusses how to save pulp for later use. It provides tips on how best to utilize the pulp and juice of certain vegetables and fruits, and describes the different types of juicers available for purchase, listing their benefits and disadvantages. All the information is in this chapter is meant to make the recipes in this book quick and easy to accomplish.

Chapter 2 dives right into the recipes themselves, offering numerous breakfast ideas that incorporate the goodness of pulp. For some reason I am always inspired to use pulp at breakfast. Perhaps it's from seeing too many commercials for high-fiber cereals when I was a kid, but pulp is great in the first meal of the day, which you will soon discover. You may begin to crave some of these breakfast recipes, such as Peaches and Cream Summer Muesli (page 33), at other times of day, which is fine, as everything in this book is so healthful.

Like breakfast foods, baked goods are another fun way to take advantage of pulp. Chapter 3 is all about using pulp in baking. As you might

1

expect, these goods tend to include wheat flour as well. Despite the bad reputation wheat has gotten in recent years, I personally don't have a problem with using wheat flour. I believe it is an excellent food for most individuals. I understand, of course, that there are a lot of people who would prefer gluten-free recipes, so you will find a few such options here.

Chapter 4 includes a number of soups, salads, and dressings. These recipes were more challenging to come up with, but the ones that made it in the book are those I liked enough to want to serve a second time. Truly, there are no recipes in this book that I don't consider special, and nothing was invented just as a way to use pulp. Every dish is a delicious meal that uses pulp to its advantage, not as a gimmick.

In Chapter 5 you will find recipes for delicious sauces, spreads, and dips. Pulp can be a wonderful base for chutneys and salsa when spiced just right. Pulp can also be made into delectable vegan spreads and pâtés that may be enjoyed on bread or crackers, or as a dip for raw veggies.

Pulp and main dishes go together like beans and rice, or cornbread and greens. Therefore, creating simple and tasty recipes for pulpy main meals was easy. Even my picky friend, who had been very skeptical about eating pulp, told me I should have made more Faux Salmon Patties (page 101) for a get-together we were attending. She wanted seconds! In Chapter 6 you will find main dishes that are satisfying, delicious, and, for my vegan readers, made without animal products.

When thinking about ways to use pulp in desserts, carrot cake is typically the first thought that comes to mind, but the array of marvelous desserts that can be made with pulp only starts there. Chapter 7 contains dessert recipes that benefit from the addition of pulp and lack of refined flours and sugar. I believe that even desserts should be healthful.

If you juice, then clearly you care about your health. If you are a healthful person, then you likely care about the health of the people for whom you cook. The recipes in this book were created without animal products or highly processed ingredients in order to make sure what you cook is as nutritious as it can be. You don't have to be vegan to enjoy the dishes in this book, though. These dishes are simply a great way to optimize your diet with some highly nutritious vegan food. I am so happy to have expanded my culinary repertoire with these recipes. They have made my diet healthier than ever. I have a feeling that when you try these meals, you will feel the same way.

1.

Prelude

If you juice, you have probably asked yourself, "What can I do with all this pulp?" If you are like me, then throwing it away seems like such a waste—and it is. Leftover pulp from juiced fruits and vegetables—what I call "juicing pulp"—can be a valued ingredient in many recipes. It can improve the texture of numerous dishes, as well as add flavor, color, dietary fiber, and nutritional value.

I've discovered many ways to use juicing pulp in my cooking over the years, and I've created dozens of recipes that actually highlight this overlooked ingredient. In addition to collecting these recipes for you in one volume, I want to offer some background information on pulp. On the following pages, you'll find a brief overview on the subject of pulp, along with some helpful guidelines for preparing, storing, and using it. Since you can't have pulp without juicing, I've also included a section on the many ways in which you may use fresh juice to enliven your everyday meals. And to help take the guesswork out of preparing these recipes, I've created a useful chart that lists the most popular fruits and vegetables along with the approximate amounts of pulp and juice they produce.

Using the pulp from juiced produce is an approach to cooking that not only lends great nutritional value and texture to dishes but also avoids waste. I've always been someone who tries to make the most of everything the earth provides. (I *really* hate wasting food.) So, welcome to my "pulp kitchen." Get ready to be wowed by this truly beneficial ingredient.

3

THE POWER OF PULP

Until recently, most people thought using the pulp from juiced produce wasn't worth the bother. "The goodness is in the juice," has been the claim by most juicing enthusiasts. The truth is that, while juice is certainly rich in "goodness," pulp has much to offer as well. Rich in fiber and nutrients, pulp offers ecological and economical advantages.

Fiber-Rich

One of the most obvious and important characteristics of pulp is that it contains fiber—the part of plant food that cannot be digested or absorbed by the body. Also known as roughage, fiber comes in two forms: soluble and insoluble. Each form is present in most plants, and each play an important role in digestion (and more).

Soluble fiber, which dissolves in water, becomes a gel-like substance that binds to the fats in food and prevents the body from absorbing them. This action helps lower levels of harmful LDL cholesterol, which can lead to heart attack, atherosclerosis, or other forms of cardiovascular disease. Soluble fiber also slows down the rate of sugar absorption, which helps regulate blood-glucose levels—this characteristic is especially beneficial to those with type 2 diabetes or metabolic syndrome—the precursor of type 2 diabetes. The following is a list of excellent sources of soluble fiber.

TOP SOURCES OF SOLUBLE FIBER			
Apples	Blackberries	Flaxseeds	Oranges
Apricots	Broccoli	Grapefruit	Pears
Bananas	Brussels sprouts	Grapes	Peas
Barley	Cabbage	Nuts	Prunes
Beans (pinto, kidney, lima, navy)	Carrots	Oat bran	Split peas
	Chia seeds	Oatmeal	Sweet potatoes
	Chickpeas	Okra	

Insoluble fiber, which does not dissolve in water, maintains its form, helping food move through the digestive tract quickly. This is the primary type of fiber found in pulp. It prevents constipation and keeps the body "regular." It also reduces the amount of time unhealthful substances stay in the body. Good sources of insoluble fiber include the following foods.

TOP SOURCES OF INSOLUBLE FIBER

Bananas	Cabbage	Lentils	Prunes
Barley	Cauliflower	Lettuces	Spinach
Broccoli	Celery	Nuts	Tomatoes
Brown rice	Corn	Onions	Wheat bran
Brussels sprouts	Green beans	Potatoes (with skin)	Whole grains
Bulgur	Kale		Whole wheat

While whole grains, beans, fruits, vegetables, nuts, and seeds all contain dietary fiber, other foods such as meat, fish, dairy products, and eggs contain no fiber at all. Although many products on store shelves contain grains—especially bread, cereal, pasta, and other baked goods—most of the fiber has been removed from these products through processing. To maximize your daily intake of fiber, try to avoid products made with refined grains and flours, and replace them with fresh whole grains.

High-fiber foods aid digestion, lower cholesterol, balance blood sugar, and promote weight control. They make us feel pleasantly full for longer periods of time and keep hunger pangs in check. They also tend to be low in calories. (This is one of the many reasons I love my vegan diet. I really enjoy eating, and the fact that I can eat pretty much all I want without gaining weight is a real bonus.)

You may be surprised to learn that 90 percent of Americans eat only about half the fiber they need for good health according to a recent article in the *Journal of Nutrition*. So, how much fiber do you need? The Institute of Medicine recommends that both children and adults consume 14 grams of fiber for every 1,000 calories of food they eat. This means that a 2,500-calorie daily intake should include at least 35 grams of fiber. Someone who eats 1,700 calories should consume approximately 24 grams, while a toddler who eats 1,300 calories would need approximately 18 grams.

There are a lot of products out there that claim to "detoxify" the body, but it seems to me that the simplest path to a "clean" body is simply to support the body's natural detoxification processes by avoiding unhealthy foods, drinking enough water, exercising, and getting enough fiber from food sources like whole grains, fresh produce, and juicing pulp.

By eating a plant-based diet and choosing whole grains and whole grain products over refined ones, your diet should contain a sufficient amount of fiber. If you find you need an added boost, adding fiber-rich juicing pulp to your dishes can provide it.

More than Just Fiber

Along with the health-enhancing qualities of dietary fiber, juicing pulp also contains a valuable assortment of nutrients and phytochemicals, which are the health-protective chemical compounds responsible for giving plant-based foods their wonderful colors, odors, and flavors. While much of the nutrient value of fruits and vegetables is found in the juice itself, the pulp contains a considerable amount as well. In fact, a study of the nutritional composition of carrot and beet pulp by Drs. B.N. Shyamala, Jr. and P. Jamuna found that "carrot and beetroot pulp wastes can be exploited for their nutrients and antioxidant components, and used for value addition in food formulations." In other words, pulp, which has been traditionally considered waste by the food industry, has enough healthful nutrients and antioxidants to enrich processed food products. Imagine how nutritious it could make unprocessed, unrefined foods!

Along with using pulp for its dietary benefits, there is an ecological advantage to this practice. It almost goes without saying that using as much of a food plant as possible is the best ecological practice. Fruits and vegetables require precious resources such as water, topsoil, and nutrients to grow, as well as physical labor for planting, cultivating, harvesting, and distributing them. Anyone who has ever grown fruits or vegetables knows how much effort it takes to bring them from seed to table. Wasting these gifts of the earth or any other natural resource is detrimental to both humans and the environment. The healthiest and happiest people I know are the ones who live, eat, and exercise wisely and mindfully.

If you garden, at some point you've probably found yourself with an overabundance of fresh vegetables—more than you could ever eat or even share. Instead of watching your bounty wither away, juice it! Even if you don't garden, when produce is in season you can get great buys at your local farmer's market or CSA (community supported agriculture). You can purchase fresh fruits and vegetables in bulk, and enormous bunches of greens—all at bargain prices. If you find you've purchased more than you can use, juice it. Take the resultant pulp and either add it to a recipe right away or freeze it for later. As you will see, there are countless ways to include pulp in your meals.

Everyday Uses

In this book, you will find lots of recipes that call for pulp. In this introductory chapter, however, I simply want to offer a few general uses for this juicing byproduct. You could:

- add fruit pulp to muesli, porridge, pie fillings, or crumbles; or blend it into sorbets or smoothies.

- add vegetable pulp to slaws or green salads, especially shredded or chopped varieties.

- add pulp to batter to keep cakes, muffins, or other baked goods moist.

- blend vegetable pulp into soups, stews, or sauces for added body.

- include pulp in your favorite veggie burgers or meatless loaves (which tend to be soft and somewhat challenging to form) for added texture and better consistency.

By no means is this list complete, of course. You'll notice that once you start using pulp in your kitchen, you will begin to come up with an even greater number of options. As an avid juicer, I usually have some pulp on hand. When I am not able to use it right away, I refrigerate it in an airtight container, where it will keep for about three days. Freezing it in freezer bag is another possibility, but doing so will change the texture of the pulp slightly.

JUICING CONSIDERATIONS

Although the focus of this book is the culinary use of juiced pulp, it is nevertheless important to touch upon a few points regarding the practice of juicing.

Choose Organic and GMO-Free

When you juice regularly, you consume large quantities of produce, so it's important to buy organic. Eating organic food goes hand in hand with a healthy diet. Organic food is grown without synthetic chemicals. By eating organic food, you will be lowering your exposure to harmful pesticide residue and avoiding genetically modified organisms, or GMOs. "Genetically modified organism" is a term used for an organism whose genes have been artificially manipulated for the purpose of creating specific traits. In regard to plants, this usually refers to a crop that has been made resistant to certain pests or herbicides. For example, GMO "Roundup Ready" corn can be doused with the herbicide known as "Roundup" to kill the unwanted weeds and not wilt a leaf, while any natural plant would wither and die after being treated with this product. This corn is said to be perfectly safe, but is it? The main genetically modified food crops at present include corn, canola, and soy. This is why buying organic soy and corn is especially important. Thankfully, the only genetically modified foods that lend themselves to juicing are crookneck squash and certain types of papaya.

In addition to its health advantages, organic food usually tastes better because it is grown in richer, healthier soil. Current research is also beginning to confirm what most organic proponents have known intuitively for years, which is that organic food is more nutritious. It's all about the soil. Rich, healthy soil creates more nutritious food than poor soil that has been chemically doused with the nutrients it requires to grow plants, which is common practice in industrial farming.

According to the United States Department of Agriculture (USDA) organic growers must:

- abstain from the application of prohibited materials (including synthetic fertilizers, pesticides, and sewage sludge) for three years prior to certification, and then continually throughout their organic licenses.

- prohibit the use of genetically modified organisms and irradiation.

- employ positive soil building, conservation, manure management, and crop rotation practices.

- avoid contamination during the processing of organic products.

- keep records of all operations.

If you must use non-organic produce on occasion, try to be sure it is not part of the Environmental Working Group's "Dirty Dozen," which is now called the "Dirty Dozen Plus," as the list has grown to include more than twelve fruits and vegetables. The list may fluctuate slightly from year to year, but it currently consists of the following items, which have been numbered from most detectable pesticides to least.

THE DIRTY DOZEN PLUS

1. Apples	**8.** Sweet bell peppers
2. Peaches	**9.** Cucumbers
3. Nectarines	**10.** Cherry tomatoes
4. Strawberries	**11.** Snap peas (imported)
5. Grapes	**12.** Potatoes
6. Celery	**13.** Hot peppers
7. Spinach	**14.** Kale and collard greens

The addition of kale and collard greens to the list is surprising and disheartening, and most likely reflects their newfound popularity and the market's attempt to keep up with it.

In opposition to the "Dirty Dozen Plus," there is a group of fruits and vegetables that are low in pesticides called the "Clean Fifteen." In order of pesticide contamination from least to most, this group is made up of the following foods.

THE CLEAN FIFTEEN

1. Avocados
2. Sweet corn
3. Pineapples
4. Cabbage
5. Sweet peas (frozen)
6. Onions
7. Asparagus
8. Mangoes
9. Papayas
10. Kiwi fruit
11. Eggplant
12. Grapefruit
13. Cantaloupe (domestic)
14. Cauliflower
15. Sweet potatoes

Keep in mind that two of the "Clean Fifteen"—corn and papayas—are crops that are frequently genetically modified. Even though certain GMO crops use fewer insecticides, they nevertheless use a greater amount of herbicide (as is the case with corn). In fact, the widespread use of "Roundup Ready" crops has led to a problematic reliance on that particular herbicide, "Roundup," also known as glyphosate. This overdependence on "Roundup" has resulted in the growth of glyphosate-resistant superweeds, which cause farmers to douse crops with even more glyphosate. In 2015, the World Health Organization declared glyphosate "probably carcinogenic to humans." Consuming a variety of pesticides or large amounts of a specific herbicide combined with GMOs—who knows which is worse? I don't think there are any scientists who know the long-term effects of either choice. I simply prefer to buy organic.

Juicing with the Seasons

My juicing produce changes with the seasons. For example, I do not juice peaches in January, but in summer, when local organic peaches are abundant and inexpensive, they are a delicious treat. Other summer juicing choices include cucumbers, celery, tomatoes, melons, parsley, and other greens. In winter, I generally use cabbage, apples, beets, carrots, garlic, and ginger. When you juice according to season, you support sustainable agricultural practices. You will also save money by buying local in-season produce.

According to Ayurvedic medicine and traditional Chinese medicine, choosing your fruits and vegetables according to season will help you sustain your body's warmth in the winter and keep yourself cool in the summer. Nature provides the foods we need at the times we need them.

CULINARY USES OF A JUICER

A juicer can greatly expand your recipe repertoire. If you already juice, knowing how to use a juicer in food preparation can help you cut down on prep time and put together meals more quickly. You can use it to grind up fruits and vegetables without getting out a blender or food processor. Although this book is mostly about pulp, the idea of using fresh juice in food preparation is so exciting and underexplored that it is worth some attention. Using freshly extracted juice in place of other liquids in recipes can provide a whole new culinary experience, yielding extraordinary results while giving your meals a huge nutritional boost. As you will soon see, the pulp and juice that come out of your juicer are excellent ways to add flavor, texture, color, and extra nutrition to your dishes.

Cooking with Juice

Almost any vegetable juice, and in some cases vegetable and fruit juice combinations, may be used to braise vegetables, tofu, or tempeh. Simply add 1/4 cup juice to the skillet when you sauté onions and garlic along with 1 tablespoon tamari and a little balsamic vinegar.

Use low-sodium tamari if you wish to limit your salt intake. Add 1 teaspoon herbes de Provence or any other culinary herbs you enjoy. Cover and cook slowly until the onions are done and most of the liquid has evaporated, adding more juice if the pan gets too dry. Sautéed onions and garlic make a delicious topping for many dishes, but other produce, such as sliced mushrooms, bell peppers, carrots, or cabbage, may also be added to the pan once the onions have been simmering for a couple of minutes.

If you are limiting your oil intake, it is still possible to make flavorful stir-fry dishes by using juice. This cooking option works a lot like braising, but it is done without oil and at a higher heat. Use any vegetables that stir-fry nicely, which include onions, broccoli, squash, bell peppers, and carrots. Use about 1/2 cup vegetable juice (of any kind of vegetable you would use in a stir-fry) and the juice of a 1-inch piece of ginger and 2 to 3 cloves of garlic. Add 2 tablespoons tamari and 1 tablespoon rice vinegar. If you'd like a sweet-sour flavor, add a bit of fruit juice such as pineapple or orange juice to the mixture.

Put the juice mixture in a wok or large skillet. If you use onions, add them first and cook them over medium heat, stirring constantly until they start to become translucent, and then add the other vegetables. Stir regularly, adding more juice (or water) to the mixture if it starts to dry out. After about three to five minutes, add a little more juice, if needed, and cover to let steam until the desired level of tenderness is achieved.

If there is still a lot of liquid left in the pan after braising or stir-frying, it can be thickened it into a sauce with some arrowroot or kuzu powder. A slightly rounded tablespoon of arrowroot or kuzu dissolved in 1/4 cup cold liquid will nicely thicken about 3/4 cup leftover cooking liquid. It must be dissolved in cold water or juice before adding it to the hot liquid, otherwise it will lump. Potato juice is also a beautiful thickener that can be used to create delicate low-calorie sauces or give body to soups. A small potato run through the juicer will make about 1/4 cup juice, which will thicken 3/4 cup liquid. Mix the potato juice into the liquid, bring to a boil, and season it as you would like. The seasoning may be a splash of tamari, some salt or miso, or any herbs or spices you wish. The potato pulp may be added to veggie burgers, casseroles, breads, or pancakes.

Fresh juice makes a beautiful food coloring. Try using freshly extracted juices to create fun and intensely colored meals sure to delight the kids. Imagine green mashed potatoes with bright pink gravy! Just remember what any artist knows: Orange and green make brown. Keep your colors clear by not blending juices of different colors together in one dish. Green juice from parsley, spinach, or other greens may be added to soups, dips, sauces, breads, mashed potatoes, or grain dishes such as polenta to give them a nutritional boost. Orange-colored juice from carrots may be used to brighten up and sweeten these same items. Red juice from beets brings neon pink to your plate and may be used in desserts, drinks, soups, sauces, dips, baked goods, and grain dishes as well. For a special party dish, take a white bean dip separated into three batches—-one colored with beet juice, one with green juice, and one with carrot juice. Lightly swirl them together in a bowl for an amazing result.

Will Cooking Destroy Nutritional Value?

Add freshly extracted juice to a recipe after you have removed the cooked portion from your heat source whenever possible, so that it may retain all its vitamins and enzymes. This may not work in every recipe, though, and as far as I'm concerned, that's fine. Cooked juice can still be highly nutritious. Minerals do not seem to be affected much by heat, and some phytonutrients are actually enhanced by it. In my opinion, the healthiest diet contains an abundance of both cooked and raw foods. If you could get your favorite vegetable-hater to consume

TOUGH TIMES

Don't like to peel broccoli stems? Juice them! Tough bits and pieces of vegetables often get thrown away. Just think of all those cabbage cores, thick stems from collards or kale, and hard ends of asparagus that have been tossed in the trash. Instead of making more garbage, juice these odds and ends and use the juice to enrich soups, sauces, stews, or any other savory dishes that call for broth.

kale by adding the juice to a cooked recipe, they would be getting a valuable dose of calcium, iron, and other nutrients that they would not be getting otherwise. Using juice to replace the liquid in both cooked and raw dishes can be a wonderful way to enrich your food.

Different Juices, Different Uses

While juicing is easy, you still have to learn the best ways to use different juices in cooking. The following is not a definitive list; it's just a few of the methods I have devised over time. I'm sure you will come up with an even greater number of creative ideas by bringing your own experience and taste to the table.

Asparagus. Juice the tough ends and add the liquid to soups or sauces, or use it to sauté the asparagus. The flavor of asparagus juice is mild, so it can also replace some of the water in rice or other grain dishes.

Beets. Add beet juice to almost anything that would look pretty in pink. Start with a tablespoon and add as much as needed for the desired color, tasting as you go to make sure you don't change the flavor of your dish too much. Try it in baked goods, blended tofu puddings or pie fillings, jams, or mashed potatoes.

Bell peppers. The juice of bell peppers can be added to sauces, soups, or stews, or added to the water used to cook grains. Red, yellow, or orange bell pepper juice is especially good in tomato based dishes, while green bell pepper juice will dull the nice red color when mixed with tomatoes.

Bok choy. Bok choy certainly grows well and may be found at a good price at the farmer's market when in season. Its juice is mild, so if you find yourself in the predicament of having too much bok choy, then juice it to create a flavorful base for soups, or to replace part of the water when cooking rice or other grains. Bok choy juice can also be frozen to use in soups or sauces later.

Broccoli stems. This juice is mild and can be used as an addition to soups or stews, or to replace part of the water when cooking rice or grains.

Cabbage. Cabbage juice is much like the juice made from broccoli stems and may be used in the same ways.

Carrot. Add to baked goods instead of milk or water, or stir into mashed potatoes for color, sweetness, and a boost of vitamins. Add carrot juice at the end of cooking to hot or cold vegetable soups, or use it in sauces.

Celery. Try adding a little celery juice to hot or cold soups after they are cooked, or use it to replace some of the water when cooking grains.

Cucumber. Use this juice to replace all or part of the liquid in cold soups or salad dressings.

Lettuce. Lettuce juice is very mild and can be included in warm or cold soups or stews, or added to the water used to cook grains or sauces.

Green juices. Juice from kale, parsley, or other greens may be used to enrich a batter or dough with calcium, iron, and phytonutrients. Like the other vegetable juices, it may also replace part of the cooking water when cooking grains, or be used in soups or stews.

Lemons. Juice a lemon with all or some of the rind still on to give a zing to salads, salad dressings, sauces, desserts, or baked goods.

Potatoes. Potato juice may be used as a thickening agent in soups or sauces.

Squash. All types of summer squash, including zucchini, yellow squash, and pattypan squash, yield mild juice that can be used to replace part of the cooking water in grains, used as a soup base, or added to baked goods.

Tomatoes. Fresh tomato juice may be added to pasta dishes, grains, soups, stews, casseroles, or sauces.

Most people who juice have tried juicing ginger and parsley, but what about herbs and spices such as lemongrass, basil, or mint? Mint juice and lemongrass juice add delightful freshness to fruit salads, salad dressings, soups, sauces, desserts, and teas. To juice mint, simply wash it and remove the leaves from the stems; but to juice lemongrass, use only the white part at the bottom. If you have too much basil on hand, try juicing it along with tomatoes. This juice may be added to soups, sauces, salad dressings, marinades, or stews.

PULP TIPS

Pulp Kitchen is a little different from most cookbooks because all the recipes use juicing pulp, and some use both pulp and juice. To save time and make the recipes easier to follow, I would like to offer a few tips.

When a recipe calls for vegetable pulp, it can be all carrot pulp or any mixture of dry pulp, including carrot, cabbage, kale, or celery with the strings picked out. Wet pulp, such as tomato or spinach, should not be used unless specified. Always consider if a pinkish color is desirable in a recipe before adding beet pulp. If a recipe calls for a specific type of pulp, it is best to use what is called for unless you are an experienced cook.

When you will need the pulp of a specific fruit or vegetable but are juicing many types of produce, juice the fruit or vegetable that will

ABOUT THE RIND

A few recipes in this book mention juicing citrus fruit with the rind. I learned this technique many years ago from "Juice Lady" Cherie Calbom, and I love the flavor it lends certain dishes. The manufacturers of some juicers, however, recommend always peeling citrus fruit before juicing, as the rind may be too taxing on the machine and could cause the motor to burn out. They may also advise against juicing citrus rind due to its bitter taste. Large quantities of citrus rind may, indeed, be too hard on certain juicers, and definitely too bitter for most recipes, but I have juiced citrus rind in small quantities for years and the results have been great. If you are concerned about your juicer's ability to juice citrus rind, simply peel citrus fruit before juicing, even if a recipe's instructions state otherwise.

yield the pulp you require first, and then collect the pulp before continuing to juice. For example, if you are juicing apple with dandelion greens and fennel and you want to make apple granola, you won't want the apple pulp to taste like dandelion greens, so juice the apple first and remove its pulp before juicing the other items. Parsley, kale, collards, and other tough greens may need a bit of help to get through the hopper of your juicer. Obviously, you never want to place your hands anywhere inside the hopper when juicing. To make things easier, juice the greens with another type of produce that can act as a plunger, such as a cucumber or a stalk of celery.

If you are saving the pulp of fruits and vegetables, always juice fruits first and remove the pulp right away, especially if you plan on juicing items such as onions, shallots, or garlic. Surely you don't want your fruit pulp tasting of onions, shallots, or garlic!

PREPPING FOR PULP

Once you try the recipes in this book, you may find yourself juicing as much for the pulp as for the juice. When saving pulp to use in recipes, there are a few general rules to keep in mind so that the pulp will be pleasant to eat.

- Always remove inedible seeds, cores, stems, and skin before juicing.

- As they are generally used in smaller quantities, herbs and spices should be juiced before fruits and vegetables. Without more juice to rinse herbs and spices out of the juicer, their flavors may stay inside the machine and be wasted. The same is true of lemons and limes.

- Cut or tear out bruised and or damaged spots.

The following list includes some of the most commonly juiced types of produce with instructions on how to prep each item to juice and save the pulp. It also has ideas on how to use these juices in recipes.

Apples. Wash and core apples, making sure not to juice the seeds, which contain arsenic. Slice apples to fit the hopper of your juicer. If there are any large pieces of skin left in pulp, discard them. Pulp may be used in fruit leathers, smoothies, porridges, mueslis, pancakes, muffins, or other baked goods.

Beets. Scrub beets and cut off tops and bottoms. Cut into chunks to fit the hopper of your juicer. Like carrot pulp, beet pulp is very versatile. It may be used in veggie burgers when the color would not be overwhelming, such as in burgers made with black or red beans. In cookies or muffins, the red beet color can be very pretty.

Broccoli stems. Broccoli stems juice nicely. Don't bother juicing the tops; they are so good to eat. If you have a large quantity of stems and want to use the pulp, it may be worth it use the pulp in a blended soup. Pulp may also be used in veggie burgers or other savory dishes, but be sure to pick out any stringy parts you might find. Feel free to mix it with other types of pulp such as carrot, cabbage, or beet.

Cabbage. Wash cabbage before juicing and remove any bruised or wilted leaves. Cut cabbage into pieces that will fit the hopper of your juicer. Cabbage pulp is milder than you might think, and it is delicious in any number of meatless burgers or loaves. It may also be used in spreads, coleslaw-type salads, or pâtés.

Carrots. Scrub carrots and remove the top and bottom parts. If carrots are large, you may have to cut them into halves to fit the hopper of your juicer. Carrot pulp is one of the most versatile types of pulp, which is good, as it is also the most common sort when you begin juicing. It may be used in sweet as well as in savory dishes. It's great in veggie burgers, faux meatballs, and veggie loaves. It also works in spreads, pâtés, and some salads, and is wonderful in breads, muffins, cookies, and cakes.

Celery. Wash celery before juicing, making sure to rinse off any dirt from the stalks. Celery pulp is great blended into soups or pâtés. It also helps make a good broth. Unless the pulp is to be blended or strained, as it would be to make a broth, pick out the strings.

Chard. Wash chard and roll big leaves to juice. Remove strings from pulp unless it is to be blended or strained. Chard does not make a lot of pulp, but it can be used in soups, stews, pâtés, and casseroles.

Citrus. If you like the flavor of citrus zest, you may leave the rind on half of one fruit when juicing produce such as oranges, tangerines, or lemons. Grapefruit and limes are best peeled, though, as their skins are very bitter. Their seeds can be quite bitter, too, and are better removed. You may add citrus pulp to mueslis, cookies, pancakes, fruit leathers, salads, or smoothies.

Coconut. Juicing coconut is something I have done repeatedly without problem, but it may be too taxing for some juicers. If you wish to juice a coconut, use a mature, not green, coconut. Poke a hole in the softest "eye" on the coconut and drain it. Strain the coconut water to be sure there are no bits of shell in it. Save the water in the fridge or drink it right away. Break the coconut open with a hammer and pry out the flesh with a screwdriver or dull knife. If you want the pulp to be pure white, peel the brown skin with a potato peeler. Cut the coconut meat into small pieces and juice them slowly. The pulp is light and delicious, and may be used in any way you would use dried or freshly grated coconut. The juice, which is really a rich coconut cream, is wonderful in curries, porridges, and desserts. If you need to store the pulp, freeze it. It may seem dry and fluffy, but it is actually moist and, unlike dried coconut, will spoil if kept too long.

Cucumber. Wash cucumber and cut into spears. Peel if waxed. You may use the pulp in salads, coleslaws, raw nut pâtés, or smoothies. Cooking with cucumber may seem strange, but the pulp may be mixed with carrot pulp or beet pulp and added to veggie burgers, faux meat balls, casseroles, or veggie loaves.

Dandelion greens. Wash greens before juicing. Pick strings out of the pulp unless it is to be blended or strained. There will not be a lot of pulp, and the pulp will be stringy, but it may be used in blended soups and pâtés. Because it is bitter, I prefer it in cooked dishes.

Fennel. Wash and cut the bulb to fit the hopper of your juicer. The stalks and part of the greens can be juiced, but they make very stringy pulp. Blend pulp into soups or smoothies, or use in a broth for an anise-like flavor.

Grapes. Wash grapes and remove stems and seeds, if any. Grape seeds, like apple seeds, contain small amounts of arsenic, and it is probably better to be safe than sorry. You may use the pulp in mueslis, cereals, fruit leathers, sorbets, or smoothies.

Kale and collards. Wash greens before juicing. Pick out any stringy parts from the pulp unless it is to be blended or used in a broth. Roll large leaves to juice. It is not necessary to remove stems. Kale and collards do not make a lot of pulp, but in savory dishes it may be combined with carrot, beet, or cabbage pulp. It may also be added to soups, stews, or green smoothies.

Mangoes. Peel, remove the seeds, and slice mangoes to fit the hopper of your juicer. Add mango pulp to desserts, sorbets, smoothies, mueslis, fruit leathers, chutneys, or sauces.

Parsley. Wash parsley before juicing. Pick out stringy parts from the pulp unless it is to be blended or strained. Parsley pulp may be used in soups, stews, potato dishes, some salads, salad dressings, sauces, casseroles, savory breads, or other baked goods.

Peaches. Wash peaches, remove the pits, and cut peaches into quarters. Pick out any large pieces of skin that may remain in the pulp. The pulp is moist and delicious. Use it in baked goods, pies, porridges, mueslis, fruit leathers, smoothies, or desserts.

Pears. Wash pears, remove cores and seeds, and slice pears into quarters. Like peach pulp, pear pulp is moist and delicious. Use it in baked goods, pies, porridges, mueslis, fruit leathers, or desserts.

VEGETABLE PULP

When a recipe calls for vegetable pulp, you can use all-carrot pulp or any mixture of dry pulp, which may include carrot, cabbage, kale, or celery with the strings picked out. When a recipe calls for vegetable juice, you can use all-carrot juice or any combination of carrot and cabbage, kale, or celery.

Pineapples. Cut off the top and bottom of the pineapple and remove the rind. Slice the fruit into spears. You can juice the core along with the flesh. Pineapple pulp is also moist and delicious. Use it in baked goods, pies, porridge, mueslis, fruit leathers, smoothies, or desserts.

Romaine lettuce. Wash lettuce and roll the leaves. Add the pulp to soups, stews, slaws, pâtés, burgers, casseroles, or smoothies.

Spinach. Wash spinach before juicing. Pick out stringy parts from the pulp, or buy baby spinach, which is not stringy. Use this pulp in soups, stews, pestos, casseroles, pâtés, or savory baked goods. It is too wet to use in burgers or recipes that need dry pulp, though.

Squash (summer). Wash squash and cut off any remaining stem. Slice to fit the hopper of your juicer. You may use the pulp in soups, stews, pâtés, or casseroles.

Strawberries. Rinse strawberries well before juicing. The tops are edible, but you may want to remove them if you wish to use the pulp. You can add the pulp to pancakes, baked goods, porridges, mueslis, fruit leathers, smoothies, or desserts.

Sunflower sprouts. Rinse sunflower sprouts well before juicing. Use the pulp in cold soups, pâtés, salads, salad dressings, or smoothies.

Tomatoes. Wash tomatoes and slice them to fit the hopper of your juicer. Pick out and discard any large pieces of skin left in the pulp. Tomato pulp is too wet to use in burgers, but it may be added to soups, stews, sauces, salad dressings, or salsas.

PULP STORAGE

Whenever you juice, you may save the pulp to use later. As mentioned earlier, you may keep it in an airtight container in the refrigerator for up to three days. It may last longer, but I generally go by the three-day rule for spoilage to be safe. The recipes in this book will seem quick and easy if you have pulp on hand. If you have to juice first in order to get pulp, you may find the process too time consuming.

TOO MUCH PULP

Regardless of best intentions, there are times when you will have more pulp on hand than you can use right away. Even if you'd rather not freeze it, you have other options other than putting it in the trash. Pulp may be fed to pets, composted, or used as food for a worm farm. Yes, a worm farm. For years my husband and I have been composting and running a worm farm. It has expanded from a small container called a "Can O' Worms," which I bought about ten years ago, to eight large plastic bins salvaged from our neighbor's trash. Worms are lovely little pets, and quite helpful in transforming vegetable waste into something useful. They will eat just about any vegetable scraps with gusto, except for onions and citrus, which they dislike strongly. Juicing pulp is their favorite treat. If worms are out of the question, compost spinners are easy to maintain, and are even suitable for use in most urban environments. The only things you need to know to compost successfully is to use half dry matter (also known as brown matter), such as dry leaves or dry grass clippings, and half fresh matter (also known as green matter), such as juicing pulp or vegetable trimmings, and to spin your compost daily.

Some writers suggest freezing pulp, but doing so does change the texture. If you know the pulp will be blended into a soup or sauce, then you may freeze it. Frozen pulp may not work as well in other recipes in this book, which were all created with fresh pulp.

PULP AND JUICE YIELDS

Most of these recipes list pulp by volume (e.g., 1/2 cup carrot pulp). Juice is also usually listed by volume. The only exception to this style occurs when ease of execution calls for simply stating the number of pieces of produce used (e.g., 1 lemon). The following chart has been provided to help you know approximately how much produce yields a certain amount of pulp or juice. But please remember that these amounts are all approximate. This guide is meant to give you a good idea of how much produce to use when following a recipe from start to finish so that you have no leftover pulp.

PULP AND JUICE CHART

PRODUCE	QUANTITY	JUICE	PULP
Apples	3 small to medium-sized	1 cup	$1/_3$ cup
Asparagus	Bottom portions of a 12-ounce bunch	$1/_3$ cup	1 tablespoon
Beets	1 medium-sized to large	$1/_2$ cup	$1/_2$ cup
Bell peppers	1 large	$3/_4$ cup	$1/_4$ cup
Bok choy	$1/_2$ large head	$1 1/_2$ cups	$1/_4$ cup
Cabbage	$1/_2$ small	$1 1/_2$	$1 1/_2$ cups
Carrots	6 medium-sized	1 cup	$1 1/_2$ cups
Celery	5 large stalks	$1 1/_3$ cup	$1/_4$ cup
Coconut	1 medium-sized	2 cups	1 cup
Collard greens	4 to 6 large leaves	$1/_2$ cup	$1/_4$ cup
Cranberries	$3 1/_2$ cups	$2/_3$ cup	$1/_2$ cup
Cucumber	1 large	1 cup	$1/_2$ cup
Grapefruit	1 large	1 cup	$1/_3$ cup
Grapes	2 cups	$3/_4$ cup	$1/_2$ cup
Lemons	1 medium-sized	$1/_4$ cup	$1/_4$ cup
Mangoes	1 medium-sized	$1/_2$ cup	3 tablespoons
Oranges	3 small to medium-sized	$2/_3$ cup	$1/_4$ cup
Peach	3 medium-sized	$1 1/_2$ cup	$2/_3$ cup
Pears	2 medium-sized	$3/_4$ cup	$1/_2$ cup
Pineapples	1 medium-sized	$1 1/_2$ cup	$1/_3$
Romaine Lettuce	1 heart	$1/_2$ cup	$1/_2$ cup
Spinach	1 bunch	$1/_3$ cup	$1/_2$ cup
Strawberries	2 cups whole	$3/_4$ cup	$1/_4$ cup
Sunflower sprouts	1 cup	$1/_4$ cup	$1/_4$ cup
Tomatoes	1 large	1 cup	$1/_2$ cup

PULP FOR PETS

The first person I knew who fed her dog pulp was "Juice Lady" Cherie Calbom. It was probably close to twenty years ago that I saw Cherie give Mackenzie, her charming little schnauzer, juicing pulp and a squirt of flax oil mixed into his dog food. The sweet little guy lived to a ripe old age. Wanting to learn more, I called my friend Laney Poier, who has a master's degree with a specialty in nutritional therapeutics for both pets and humans. Laney has a passion for providing the best nutrition possible for pets, and knows more about feeding them than anyone I know.

According to Laney, pulp is good for dogs, although for some dogs with delicate digestion or allergies it may be too harsh. She told me that dogs react very quickly to foods that do not agree with them, so if you introduce any new food to a dog, keep an eye out to make sure it is tolerated. When adding fruit or vegetable pulp to homemade or commercial pet food, simply go easy and add small amounts. Your pets will let you know how much of it they want to eat. Animals that eat fruits, vegetables, or seeds in nature tend to love pulp. Bunnies, hamsters, and birds all do well with fruit or vegetable pulp added to their diets.

Pulp amounts will vary depending on your juicer and the produce. Some juicers make a dryer pulp than others, and this will create a pulp that takes up less space. And, as I'm sure you are aware, the juiciness of fruits and vegetables fluctuates according to season and variety.

EQUIPMENT

A juicer, of course, is required to make these recipes. Presently, there are three main types of juicers on the market: centrifugal juicers, masticating juicers, and twin-gear juicers. Centrifugal juicers are perhaps the most popular and widely available. They are usually the most affordable option as well. These machines use a rotating blade to cut the produce, which is then forced against the holes of a surrounding mesh basket by the rapid spinning motion. The juice is strained through the strainer and the pulp is left behind. Centrifugal juicers are fast and easy to use and clean.

Instead of chopping the fruit or veggies, masticating juicers crunch the produce into a pulp using a single auger, or drill, inside a small tube. The auger turns the food slowly and crushes it against the walls of the tube, extracting the juice. Due to their rate of action, masticating juicers are also known as slow juicers. This slow process, however, may yield slightly more juice and a dryer pulp than centrifugal juicers tend to make.

Twin-gear juicers, also called triturating juicers, are typically the most expensive juicers on the market. They grind the produce between two interlocking gears, extruding the juice and creating a very dry pulp. These juicers are particularly good at juicing leafy greens. While this type of juicer may have the highest output of juice of the three, it is also the slowest mechanism. These machines also take a little more time to clean after use.

Some people use hydraulic presses or manual juicers to juice their produce, but these methods would not suit the requirements of the recipes in this book very well. Ultimately, the best juicer for you is the one you actually use. It goes without saying that a centrifugal juicer is faster than the others, which may mean you won't dread using it. It also produces a pulp that is a bit wetter than the others, which may be a better option in some of these recipes than a pulp that is too dry, but the pulp that comes from a masticating juicer works perfectly well in these dishes. In fact, the recipes in this book were created using a Champion masticating juicer. Twin-gear juicers, however, result in a pulp that is very dry—perhaps too dry for the purposes of this book.

Other equipment used to make these recipes is standard in most well-equipped kitchens. A blender or food processor will sometimes be used in conjunction with your juicer. If you have a high-powered blender such as a Vitamix, it will make blended recipes a lot easier to manage, negating the need for a food processor. You will also need a good knife, cutting board, and pots and pans. (If you do not have the recommended pots and pans, use the closest approximations on hand.) The only unusual kitchen item found in some of these recipes is a dehydrator—although you will be given oven instructions as an alternative to using a dehydrator whenever possible.

2.

The Breakfast Situation

Eating a high-fiber breakfast is easy to do in a pulp kitchen. Carrot pulp or almost any fruit pulp may be added to porridges or mueslis to increase fiber content, nutrition, and flavor. Virtually any grain that is cooked until soft and served for breakfast may be considered porridge, but the most common version would be oatmeal. There are several porridge recipes in this book, but you don't need to follow only those found here to take advantage of pulp's benefits. Adding pulp to any oatmeal or porridge will do the trick. To make porridge even yummier, add spices such as cinnamon, cardamom, cloves, or allspice, and top it with fresh fruit and some nondairy yogurt or milk. This same advice also holds true for muesli.

Created as an ideal breakfast by Swiss doctor Maximilian Bircher-Benner around 1900, muesli consists of soaked oats, fruit, seeds, nuts, and often grated apple. When you make your own, you can mix and match fresh or dried fruit, nuts, seeds, soaked grains, and pulp. I usually use rolled oats for muesli, grinding them in the blender so that they soak up liquid quickly. The grains of the muesli recipes in this book may be soaked overnight, so you could always make muesli in the afternoon or evening for a ready-to-eat breakfast the next day. Use any nondairy milk to soak the grains of the muesli. I prefer unsweetened soy milk because it is high in protein. If you would prefer not to use milk, any freshly extracted fruit juice or simply water would work, too. If the muesli comes out too thick, just add a little milk, juice, or water.

Are you are looking for something other than cereal in the morning? Pancakes made with pulp are a tasty breakfast option. By mixing carrot pulp or fruit pulp with wheat, spelt, faro, or kamut, you can make delicious pancakes. If you are a vegan who misses the traditional eggs and sausage wake-up call, then my tofu scramble and faux sausage are for you. Both recipes include nutritious pulp, and both recipes are amazing.

Breakfast is a great opportunity to get creative in the kitchen because not much can go very wrong. If you'd rather not be so bold, though, you can follow any of the recipes in this chapter with the utmost confidence.

APPLE OATMEAL

This dish is easy to prepare, wonderfully satisfying, and extremely nutritious. Try it topped with unsweetened nondairy yogurt, ground flax seeds, and fresh blueberries for a boost of flavor, nutrients, and fiber. It is the perfect way to warm up on a chilly morning.

Yield: 4 Servings

1 cup rolled oats	3 cups water
1/2 cup apple pulp	10 whole cloves
1/4 cup raisins	1 cinnamon stick

1. In a 2^1/$_2$-quart saucepan, combine the rolled oats, apple pulp, raisins, water, cloves, and cinnamon stick. Cover and bring to a boil. Reduce the heat and simmer for 3 to 5 minutes.

2. Remove from heat and allow the oatmeal to sit for 5 minutes. Remove the cinnamon stick before serving.

RAW CRANBERRY-
APPLE SAUCE

Make this versatile dish during the holiday season, when antioxidant-rich cranberries are abundant. If you have never tried the flavors of cranberry and apple together, you are in for a treat! Use a sweet variety of apple in this recipe and let your taste buds sing.

Yield: 2 Cups

$2/_3$ cup apple juice

$2/_3$ cup apple pulp

$1/_2$ cup cranberry pulp

$1/_2$ cup finely chopped dried figs

$1/_3$ cup chopped walnuts

1. In a medium-sized mixing bowl, combine the apple juice, apple pulp, cranberry pulp, dried figs, and walnuts. Mix well.

2. Serve this sauce piled high on toast or stirred into plain cooked oatmeal.

For a change . . .

Serve this dish in place of traditional cranberry sauce at your holiday dinner. If you'd like a sweeter sauce, add a few drops Stevia or 1 tablespoon maple syrup. You could also add spices such as freshly grated ginger, ground allspice, cloves, or cardamom.

That's All You Had to Say

Green juices are always improved by the addition of 1/4 lemon with the peel, which you may juice along with the other ingredients.

PULP PORRIDGE

A houseguest of mine was amazed by how good this meal was and said he liked it a lot better than ordinary oatmeal. Put it on to cook as soon as you wake up and let it simmer while you get ready for your day. Over low heat, it should not stick, so you won't have to stir it while it is cooking.

Yield: 4 Servings

2 to 3 medium-sized apples, diced

3 cups water

1 cup rolled oats

1 cup carrot pulp

$^1/_4$ cup dried shredded coconut

$^1/_4$ cup raisins

$^1/_2$ teaspoon coriander

1 tablespoon coconut butter

1 teaspoon vanilla extract

1. In a $2^1/_2$-quart saucepan, combine the apples and water. Cover and bring to a boil.

2. Add the rolled oats, carrot pulp, shredded coconut, raisins, and coriander to the saucepan. Stir and cover. Reduce the heat to low and cook for 20 to 30 minutes. Remove from heat and allow oatmeal to sit for 5 minutes.

3. Stir in the coconut butter and vanilla extract. Serve warm.

Helpful Tip

If you are in a hurry, simmer the apples in the water for about 5 minutes before adding the other ingredients. Add the remaining ingredients except the coconut butter and vanilla extract. Mix well and bring to a boil. Cover and cook over medium heat for about 5 minutes, stirring occasionally.

NUT AND SEED MEUSLI WITH LEMON AND BLUEBERRIES

The lemon, which is juiced along with its peel, gives this muesli a refreshing flavor, while the blended cashews create a rich cream that makes it irresistible.

Yield: 2 to 3 Servings

3 to 4 large apples	2 tablespoons chia seeds
$1/2$ lemon, cut into 2 wedges, seeded, and left unpeeled	$1/4$ cup cashews
1 cup rolled oats	1 cup unsweetened nondairy milk or water
$1/4$ cup pumpkin seeds	1 to 2 cups blueberries (fresh or frozen)

1. Juice the apples and lemon wedges. Reserve the juice and the pulp.

2. In a blender, combine the rolled oats and pumpkin seeds. Coarsely·grind and transfer to a large mixing bowl.

3. Add the reserved apple and lemon pulp and chia seeds to the bowl. Set aside.

4. In the blender, combine the apple and lemon juice, cashews, and milk. Blend until smooth and creamy.

5. Add the cashew mixture to the bowl and stir. Add the blueberries and allow the muesli to sit for at least 10 minutes. If it becomes too thick, add more milk. Serve as desired.

ORANGE AND GINGER WINTER MUESLI

The spices used in this recipe lend the dish a feeling of gentle warming. As oranges ripen in winter and apples store well, the availability of high quality fresh fruit should not be a problem when it gets cold outside.

Yield: 2 to 3 Servings

2 medium-sized apples, cored and cut into wedges

1 large orange, cut into 4 to 6 wedges, seeded, and peeled, leaving 1 wedge unpeeled for pulp.

1/2-inch piece ginger, peeled

1/4 cup flax seeds

1 cup rolled oats

1/4 cup raisins

1 teaspoon ground cinnamon

1/4 teaspoon ground cloves

1/2 cup nondairy milk

1. Juice the apples, orange, and ginger. Transfer the juice and pulp to a large mixing bowl.

2. In a blender, place the flax seeds and grind into a powder. Add the ground seeds to the bowl.

3. In the blender, combine the rolled oats, raisins, cinnamon, and cloves. Coarsely grind and transfer to the bowl.

4. Add the milk to the bowl and mix well. Allow the muesli to sit for at least 10 minutes. If it becomes too thick, add more milk. Serve as desired.

For a Change . . .

If you would like a hot cereal, gently heat the milk before you add it to the oat mixture. If you would like to make this dish more appropriate for warm weather, omit the cinnamon, ginger, and cloves, and use 1 teaspoon ground fennel and 1/2 teaspoon ground cardamom instead.

PEACHES AND CREAM SUMMER MUESLI

This muesli is delicious enough to wake up early for, so don't sleep in or you might not get any!

Yield: 3 to 4 Servings

1¹/₂ cups rolled oats

¹/₃ cup almonds

¹/₃ cups chia seeds

1 cup apple juice

1 cup peach juice

¹/₂ cup peach pulp or a combination of apple pulp and peach pulp

2 cups blueberries

2 peaches, diced

1 cup nondairy milk

1 teaspoon vanilla extract

1. In a blender, combine the rolled oats and almonds. Coarsely grind and transfer to a large mixing bowl.

2. Add the chia seeds, apple juice, peach juice, peach pulp, blueberries, peaches, milk, and vanilla extract to the bowl. Allow the muesli to sit for at least 10 minutes. If it becomes too thick, add more milk. Serve as desired.

The Difference is Huge

Keep your colors clear. Juice and pulp can have intense colors, so use them to your advantage. Avoid mixing colors that look unappetizing in combination. For example, orange or red combined with green results in brown, which can be rather unappealing to the eye. Use warm-colored juices and pulps together, such as carrot, beet, and tomato; and use cool colors together, such as green veggies and blueberries.

ORANGE GRANOLA

This granola is not too sweet, so try it with fresh fruit and your favorite yogurt. I like the taste of orange peel because it reminds me of marmalade, so I leave the peel intact on one wedge when juicing the orange. If you don't like this particularly bitter-sweet flavor, peel the entire orange before juicing.

Yield: 13 Servings

3 cups rolled oats	1 cup dried apricots or pitted dates
$1^1/_2$ cup orange juice	
$^2/_3$ cup orange pulp	$^1/_4$ cup coconut oil
$^1/_2$ cup almonds	$^1/_4$ cup maple syrup
$^1/_2$ cup pumpkin seeds or sunflower seeds	1 tablespoon vanilla extract
	$^1/_2$ cup dried shredded coconut

1. Preheat the oven to 350°F.

2. In a medium-sized mixing bowl, combine the rolled oats, orange juice, and orange pulp. Cover and let soak for about 6 hours or overnight.

3. In a small mixing bowl, combine the almonds and pumpkin seeds. Cover with water and let soak for about 6 hours or overnight. Drain.

4. In a food processor, combine half the oat mixture and the almonds and pumpkin seeds. Grind coarsely and transfer to a large mixing bowl.

5. In the food processor, combine the remaining oat mixture and the apricots. Process, adding the coconut oil, maple syrup, and vanilla extract to the machine as it is running. Transfer to the large bowl and add the shredded coconut. Mix well.

6. On an 18-x-13-inch baking sheet, spread the mixture in a thin layer. Bake for about 20 minutes. Remove the granola from the oven and stir. Reduce the heat to 300°F and bake for another 20 minutes, or until golden brown. Turn off the heat and let the granola cool in the oven for about 30 minutes, or until it is dry and crisp.

7. Let the granola sit at room temperature to cool completely before transferring it to an airtight container and storing it in the refrigerator.

For a Change . . .

Instead of baking the granola, you could prepare it in a dehydrator by placing the mixture on ParaFlexx dehydrator trays or mesh trays and dehydrating it for about 8 hours, or until crispy.

GRAPE GRANOLA

The fresh grape juice, grape pulp, and raisins make this crispy granola plenty sweet, but if you want it to be even sweeter, you could always add a few drops of liquid Stevia.

Yield: 13 Servings

3 cups rolled oats	$1/2$ cup pumpkin seeds
1 cup grape juice	$1/2$ cup flax seeds
$1/2$ cup grape pulp	2 teaspoons ground cinnamon
$1/3$ cup coconut oil	1 cup raisins

1. Preheat the oven to 300°F.

2. In a large mixing bowl, combine the rolled oats, grape juice, grape pulp, coconut oil, pumpkin seeds, flax seeds, and cinnamon. Mix well.

3. On two 18-x-13-inch baking sheets, spread the mixture in a thin layer.

4. Bake for about 1 hour, stirring occasionally, or until the mixture begins to brown. Turn off the heat and let the granola cool in the oven for about 30 minutes, or until it is dry and crisp.

5. Add the raisins to the granola. Mix well and let the granola sit at room temperature to cool completely before transferring it to an airtight container and storing it in the refrigerator.

For a Change . . .

Instead of the flax seeds and raisins, use $1/2$ cup dried shredded coconut and 1 cup chopped pitted dates.

ORANGE AND CARROT BREAKFAST CORN CAKES

These crispy gluten-free cakes make a nice weekend breakfast when served with fruit salad and your favorite yogurt.

Yield: 12 Pancakes

1 cup cornmeal

2 tablespoons egg replacer

2 teaspoons baking powder

$1/2$ teaspoon baking soda

$1/4$ cup orange juice

1 tablespoon grated orange zest

$1^1/_4$ cup carrot pulp

$1/4$ cup raisins

1 cup nondairy milk or water

3 tablespoons coconut oil, or as needed

1. In a large mixing bowl, combine the cornmeal, egg replacer, baking powder, and baking soda. Mix well. Add the orange juice, orange zest, carrot pulp, raisins, and milk. Mix again until thick batter forms.

2. In a 12-inch skillet, heat 1 tablespoon coconut oil over medium-low heat. Drop 4 heaping tablespoons of batter separately onto the skillet, leaving enough space between tablespoons to flatten each drop with the back of the spoon.

3. Cook the pancakes for 3 to 4 minutes, or until the bottoms have become golden brown. Flip the pancakes and cook for another 3 to 4 minutes. Repeat steps 2 and 3 until all the batter has been used. Serve warm.

Helpful Tip

Egg replacer may be purchased at most health food stores.

APPLE PULP PANCAKES

These pancakes are slightly sweet, delightfully crispy, and definitely delicious.

Yield: 12 Pancakes

2 cups whole wheat pastry flour

2 teaspoons baking powder

$1/_2$ teaspoon baking soda

$1^1/_4$ cup water

1 cup soy milk or water

$1/_2$ cup apple juice

$1/_2$ cup apple pulp

2 tablespoons ground flax seeds

1 tablespoon apple cider vinegar

3 tablespoons coconut oil, or as needed

1. In a large mixing bowl, combine the flour, baking powder, and baking soda. Mix well.

2. In another large mixing bowl, combine the water, milk, apple juice, apple pulp, flax seeds, and apple cider vinegar. Mix well.

3. Add the wet ingredients to the dry ingredients. Mix until thick batter forms.

4. In a 12-inch skillet, heat 1 tablespoon coconut oil over medium-low heat. Drop 4 heaping tablespoons of batter separately onto the skillet, leaving enough space between tablespoons to flatten each drop with the back of the spoon.

5. Cook the pancakes for 3 to 4 minutes, or until the bottoms have become golden brown. Flip the pancakes and cook for another 3 to 4 minutes. Repeat steps 4 and 5 until all the batter has been used. Serve warm.

PULP SOYSAGE

These little patties are made with some of the same spices used in sausage. They are fantastic served with Scrambled Pulp Tofu (page 39) and roasted potatoes for brunch, but I have also served them with vegetable curry for dinner.

Yield: 8 Patties

2 tablespoons flax seeds

1 cup vegetable pulp

1 cup cooked quinoa

8 ounces extra-firm tofu, mashed

$1/4$ cup minced onion

1 stalk celery, minced

2 to 3 cloves garlic, pressed

$1^1/2$ teaspoons whole fennel seeds, toasted in a dry skillet

$1^1/2$ teaspoons sage

1 tablespoon tamari

$1/2$ teaspoon white pepper

$1/4$ teaspoon freshly ground black pepper, or to taste

$1/2$ teaspoon salt, or to taste

2 tablespoons olive oil, divided

1. Place the flax seeds in a blender. Grind them into a fine powder. Transfer to a large mixing bowl.

2. Add the pulp, quinoa, tofu, onion, celery, garlic, fennel seeds, sage, tamari, white pepper, black pepper, and salt to the bowl. Mix well, using your hands. Shape the mixture into 8 patties of equal size.

3. In a 12-inch skillet, heat 1 tablespoon olive oil over medium heat. Add 4 patties to the skillet and cook for about 5 minutes, or until each patty is brown on the bottom. Flip the patties and cook for another 5 minutes, or until crispy brown. Repeat step 3 with the remaining patties.

SCRAMBLED PULP TOFU

This is an easy recipe that many people enjoy as a high-protein vegan breakfast or dinner. Almost any vegetable that can be sautéed may be added. Serve this dish with roasted potatoes or whole grain toast. If you have it for dinner, try it with a green salad.

Yield: 3 to 4 Servings

2 tablespoons olive oil

1 cup chopped onions

1 cup chopped celery

1 cup vegetable pulp

1 pound firm tofu, mashed or crumbled

1 tablespoon mild curry powder

1 teaspoon salt

1. In a 12-inch skillet heat the olive oil over medium heat. Add the onions and celery to the skillet. Sauté for about 5 minutes.

2. Add the vegetable pulp to the skillet. Cover and cook for another 5 minutes.

3. Add the tofu, curry powder, and salt to the skillet. Stir well. Cook for 3 to 4 minutes more. Serve immediately.

For a Change . . .

Instead of celery, use carrots, zucchini matchsticks, sliced bell pepper, or sliced mushrooms. If you don't care for curry, just use a pinch of turmeric to give this dish a yellow tint, and season it simply with salt, pepper, and some fresh parsley, basil, or rosemary. Top everything with halved or quartered cherry or grape tomatoes.

APPLE QUINOA
BREAKFAST BURGERS

These are actually croquettes, not burgers, but my husband named them, so why not keep this catchy title? This recipe makes a high-protein vegan breakfast and is a great way to use leftover cooked quinoa.

Yield: 4 Burgers

1 cup cooked quinoa	2 tablespoons crunchy peanut butter
$3/_4$ cup apple pulp	
$1/_4$ cup pitted dates	1 to 2 tablespoons coconut oil

1. In a food processor, combine the quinoa, apple pulp, dates, and peanut butter. Process until the mixture becomes sticky enough to hold together.

2. Shape the mixture into 4 patties of equal size.

3. In a 12-inch skillet, heat the coconut oil over medium heat. Add the patties to the skillet and cook for about 5 minutes, or until each patty is brown on the bottom. Flip the patties and cook for another 5 minutes, or until crispy brown.

That's All You Had to Say

You can cook, and don't let anybody tell you otherwise! We have been brainwashed by the food industry for decades to believe that only the talented few can be good cooks. You may not be a gifted chef, but anyone can take fresh high-quality ingredients and turn them into delicious meals.

3.

It's the One That Says "Breads, Muffins, Crackers"

Adding pulp to baked goods enriches them with fiber and nutrients. The best part is that it is so easy to hide pulp inside breads, muffins, and crackers. Another advantage of using pulp is that it adds moistness to a recipe, so even whole grain bread may achieve a pleasant texture without the addition of white flour. If you carefully follow the recipes in this chapter, you will meet with positive results, and if ever you want to experiment, simply remember that less is more. Don't overdo it on the pulp, as doing so will lead to a gooey outcome. In addition, when working with pulp in baked goods, keep in mind that batter containing pulp will appear thicker than batter without it.

To make truly high-quality baked goods, freshly ground flour is the way to go. While this flour may not be available at your local chain grocery store, it may be purchased online from small mills that will ship it straight to your door. Another way to make the freshest and healthiest baked goods possible is to buy new-crop whole grains from a reputable source and grind them to make your own flour at home, which can be done with an electric mill or a Vitamix blender. With a food processor or Vitamix you can even make sprouted breads, a few recipes for which you will find in this chapter. Whole grains become rancid easily, though, so it is important to store all whole grain flour in the refrigerator or freezer to prevent this from happening.

I hope you enjoy these breads, muffins, and crackers. I've even added a couple of crust recipes to use with a number of meals found later on in this book, or whenever you might need a good crust.

Remember that the best way to enjoy these items is freshly made. If you cannot eat your baked goods on the day you bake them, then be sure to freeze them (slice bread before freezing it) to keep them as wholesome as the day they came out of the oven.

APPLE CHIA CINNAMON MUFFINS

These flavorful whole grain muffins are sweetened with only fruit and Stevia. The pulp allows them to be moist without the added fat.

Yield: 12 Muffins

1^1/$_2$ cups apple juice	2 teaspoons baking powder
1 cup nondairy milk	^{1}/$_2$ teaspoon baking soda
^{1}/$_3$ cup chia seeds	1 tablespoon cinnamon
^{1}/$_2$ cup apple pulp	1 cup raisins
2 cups whole grain spelt flour or whole wheat pastry flour	

1. Preheat the oven to 350°F. Grease a 12-cup muffin pan with coconut oil and sprinkle it with flour. Set aside.

2. In a large mixing bowl, combine the apple juice and milk. Stir in the chia seeds and let sit for 10 minutes, or until the mixture becomes gelatinous. Add the apple pulp and mix again.

3. In another large mixing bowl, combine the spelt flour, baking powder, baking soda, and cinnamon. Mix well. Stir in the raisins. Mix until the raisins are evenly distributed throughout the mixture.

4. Add the dry ingredients to the wet ingredients. Mix just enough to combine the ingredients completely.

5. Divide the batter evenly among the prepared muffin cups. Bake for 40 minutes, or until a toothpick inserted in the center of a muffin comes out clean.

CARROT MUFFINS

Not only are these delicious fat-free muffins made with whole wheat, but they also get their sweetness from carrot juice and raisins, so you don't have to feel guilty when you enjoy them.

Yield: 12 Muffins

2 cups whole wheat pastry flour

1 tablespoon cinnamon, or to taste

2 teaspoons baking powder

$1/2$ teaspoon baking soda

1 cup raisins

1 cup carrot pulp

$1^1/4$ cup carrot juice

$1/2$ cup mashed firm silken tofu

1 tablespoon apple cider vinegar

1. Preheat the oven to 350°F. Grease a 12-cup muffin pan with coconut oil and sprinkle it with flour. Set aside.

2. In a large mixing bowl, combine the flour, cinnamon, baking powder, and baking soda. Mix well. Stir in the raisins and carrot pulp. Mix until the raisins and pulp are evenly distributed throughout the mixture.

3. In a blender, combine the carrot juice, tofu, and apple cider vinegar. Blend until smooth.

4. Add the wet ingredients to the dry ingredients. Mix well until batter forms, but do not overmix.

5. Divide the batter evenly among the prepared muffin cups. Bake for 20 minutes, or until a toothpick inserted in the center of a muffin comes out clean.

For a Change . . .

Instead of carrot juice and pulp, try using apple juice and pulp, or beet juice and pulp, or a combination of the two.

VEGGIE CORN MUFFINS

These savory gluten-free muffins go well with a spicy bean soup for a simple lunch. Check the sundried tomatoes you are using. If they contain salt, the batter may not need the added salt. If you use beet pulp, it will make the muffins pink on top!

Yield: 12 Muffins

$1^1/_2$ cup cornmeal

1 teaspoon baking powder

$1/_2$ teaspoon baking soda

$1/_4$ teaspoon salt

1 cup corn, fresh or frozen

1 cup vegetable pulp

$1/_3$ cup coarsely chopped sundried tomatoes

$1/_4$ cup dried onion flakes

$1/_2$ cup water

$1/_2$ cup firm silken tofu, mashed

2 tablespoons apple cider vinegar

1. Preheat the oven to 350°F. Grease a 12-cup muffin pan with coconut oil and sprinkle it with flour. Set aside.

2. In a large mixing bowl, combine the cornmeal, baking powder, baking soda, and salt. Mix well.

3. Add the corn, vegetable pulp, sundried tomatoes, and onion flakes to the large mixing bowl. Mix again, using your hands if necessary, until the pulp is evenly distributed throughout the mixture.

4. In a blender, combine the water, tofu, and apple cider vinegar. Blend until creamy. Add the wet ingredients to the dry ingredients. Mix well until batter forms.

5. Divide the batter evenly among the prepared muffin cups. Bake for 30 minutes, or until a toothpick inserted in the center of a muffin comes out clean.

CARROT CHAPATIS

This South Asian flatbread is best when eaten immediately after cooking. I use coarsely ground heirloom red fife flour to make this quick and easy bread, but any whole wheat flour will do. The carrot pulp will keep the chapatis moist and pliable, and if you make this recipe with carrot juice instead of water, the chapatis will taste slightly sweet.

Yield: 6 Chapatis

1 cup whole wheat flour	**$1/2$ cup carrot pulp**
$1/4$ teaspoon salt	$1/2$ cup water or carrot juice

1. In a medium-sized mixing bowl, combine the flour, salt, and carrot pulp. Mix well. Stir in the water.

2. Sprinkle your work surface with flour and knead the dough for about 5 minutes, or until it is somewhat firm and elastic, kneading in extra flour if necessary.

3. Pinch off a piece of dough the size of a golf ball. Using your hands, roll the piece of dough into a smooth ball. Flatten the ball between your palms and place it on the floured surface.

4. Using a rolling pin, roll the piece of dough until it is approximately 6 inches in diameter, sprinkling the work surface and the chapati with flour as needed.

5. In a 12-inch dry skillet over medium-high heat, cook the chapati until it starts to get brown flecks on the bottom. Turn it over and cook the other side, pressing down with a spatula. This should cause the chapati to puff up. Transfer the chapati to a plate and cover it with a clean dish towel to keep it warm.

6. Repeat steps 3, 4, and 5 until all the dough has been used.

DEHYDRATED FLAX CRACKERS

These flax crackers are extremely popular with people on raw-food diets, but you will need an Excalibur dehydrator to make them. If you don't have one, use the recipe for Baked Flax Crackers (page 47) instead. These crackers keep well in a covered container in the refrigerator.

Yield: 64 Crackers

2 cups flax seeds	3 cloves garlic, pressed
4 cups water	1 tablespoon balsamic vinegar
1 cup carrot pulp	2 teaspoons thyme
1 cup minced onion	1 teaspoon salt

1. In a large mixing bowl, combine the flax seeds and water. Cover and set aside for 4 to 6 hours or overnight.

2. Add the carrot pulp, onion, garlic, balsamic vinegar, thyme, and salt to the large mixing bowl. Mix well.

3. On 4 ParaFlexx dehydrator sheets or mesh screens covered with parchment paper, spread the mixture as thinly as you can without creating holes using your hands or a rubber spatula. Keep your hands or the spatula wet so it will be easier to spread.

4. Dehydrate the sheets at 105°F for about 4 to 6 hours, or until the mixture is firm. Flip them over. (If you are using parchment, peel it off.) Score the mixture with a knife so that you have 16 crackers on each sheet.

5. Continue dehydrating the crackers for 12 to 24 hours, or until very crisp. Allow the crackers to cool completely and store them in an airtight container in the refrigerator.

Helpful Tip

Keep a bowl of water next to you to you as you work. It will make wetting your hands or the spatula easy to do as you prepare the crackers.

BAKED FLAX CRACKERS

*A friend wanted to try my Dehydrated Flax Crackers recipe (page 46)
but didn't have a dehydrator, so I decided to add flour to the ingredients
and turn the crackers into baked goods. This recipe makes a large
quantity of crackers, but thankfully they store well in the refrigerator.*

Yield: 100 Crackers

2 cups flax seeds	3 cloves garlic, pressed
4 cups water	1 tablespoon balsamic vinegar
1 cup whole wheat flour	2 teaspoons thyme
1 cup carrot pulp	1 teaspoon salt
1 cup minced onion	

1. Preheat the oven to 350°F.

2. In a large mixing bowl, combine the flax seeds and water. Cover and set aside for 4 to 6 hours or overnight.

3. Add the flour, carrot pulp, onion, garlic, balsamic vinegar, thyme, and salt to the large mixing bowl. Mix well.

4. Generously grease four 18-x-13-inch baking sheets with olive or coconut oil and then dust them with flour. Drop the batter by the heaping teaspoon onto the prepared baking sheets. Dip the teaspoon in water and use it flatten out each cracker as thinly you can. You should have about 25 crackers on each baking sheet.

5. Bake the crackers for about 25 minutes, or until they are firm enough to flip. Flip them over and continue baking for another 25 minutes, or until they are crisp. If they are still not crisp, turn off the oven and leave them inside until cool. If they are still not crisp, bake for a few minutes more. Once done, allow the crackers to cool completely before storing them in an airtight container in the refrigerator.

Helpful Tip

Change the position of the baking sheets in the oven if the crackers are baking unevenly.

RAW SPINACH TORTILLAS

I got this recipe from my friend Marina Sommers, founder of Nutritious You. Marina has a talent for making raw food look and taste so good that everyone who tries her dishes cannot help but love them. You will need an Excalibur dehydrator to make this recipe.

Yield: 12 Tortillas

$1^1/_8$ cup carrot pulp

$1^1/_2$ cup coarsely chopped bell pepper

5 ounces spinach

$1^1/_2$ tablespoons lime juice

2 teaspoons chili powder

$^1/_2$ teaspoon salt, or to taste

$1^1/_4$ teaspoons cumin

2 tablespoons olive oil

$1^1/_8$ cup golden flax seeds

1. In a food processor, combine the carrot pulp, bell pepper, spinach, lime juice, chili powder, salt, cumin, and olive oil. Transfer to a large mixing bowl. Process until creamy.

2. In the food processor, grind the flax seeds into a fine powder. Add the ground flax seeds to the large mixing bowl. Mix well.

3. Lightly grease a ParaFlexx dehydrator sheet with olive oil. Add 2 tablespoons of the mixture to the sheet in a mound. Repeat until there are 4 separate mounds.

4. Lightly grease another ParaFlexx dehydrator sheet with olive oil and place it on top of the mounds of the mixture. Using the bottom of a glass pie plate, press each mound flat. Repeat steps 2 and 3 until all the mixture has been used.

5. Dehydrate the sheets at 145°F for 90 minutes. Flip the tortillas off the ParaFlexx and onto the screens than come with the dehydrator. Dehydrate the tortillas for an additional 30 to 60 minutes, or until dry to the touch but still flexible.

SPINACH TORTILLA CHIPS

This is essentially the same recipe as Raw Spinach Tortillas (page 48), except that these instructions allow you to make tortilla chips.

Yield: 120 Chips

$1^1/_8$ cup carrot pulp

$1^1/_2$ cup coarsely chopped bell pepper

5 ounces spinach

$1^1/_2$ tablespoons lime juice

2 teaspoons chili powder

$^1/_2$ teaspoon salt, or to taste

$1^1/_4$ teaspoons cumin

2 tablespoons olive oil

$1^1/_8$ cup golden flax seeds

1. In a food processor, combine the carrot pulp, bell pepper, spinach, lime juice, chili powder, salt, cumin, and olive oil. Process until creamy. Transfer to a large mixing bowl.

2. In the food processor, grind the flax seeds into a fine powder. Add the ground flax seeds to the large mixing bowl. Mix well.

3. Lightly grease 6 ParaFlexx dehydrator sheets with olive oil. Add about $1^1/_2$ cups of the mixture to each the sheet. Lightly grease 6 other ParaFlexx dehydrator sheets with olive oil and place one on top of each sheet of mixture. Using a rolling pin, roll out the mixture to the edges of each sheet.

4. Score the mixture with a knife so that you have 20 chips on each sheet.

5. Dehydrate the mixture at 145°F for 90 minutes. Lower the temperature to 115°F and continue to dehydrate for an additional 25 minutes, or until dry and very crisp.

IS WHEAT GUILTY?

Wheat has gotten a bad rap these past few years. In particular, the protein known as gluten, which is found in wheat and other grains, has come under intense criticism. In its defense, wheat has been considered the "staff of life" since the advent of agriculture. It is a very good source of dietary fiber, manganese, and magnesium. In a vegetarian or vegan diet, wheat is also a good source of protein when eaten as part of a varied diet. Whole wheat slows the assimilation of sugar by the body, which, in turn, helps prevent metabolic syndrome, the precursor of type 2 diabetes. So, what's the problem? The fact is that there are a small percentage of individuals for whom the consumption of gluten can have negative effects. These people need to avoid any foods that contain even small amounts of gluten. Most people, however, can thrive on a diet that includes whole wheat and other whole grains, provided those grains are of high quality.

Aside from biological intolerance to gluten or an allergy to wheat, another major problem with wheat is the fact that most wheat is refined, which strips it of its bran and germ, leaving it with only a fraction of the nutrition it had in its natural state. Refining wheat allows it to last for a long time without spoiling. Even in health food stores, many of the baked goods that contain wheat are made with refined wheat. Add sugar to refined wheat and you have a product that contains lots of empty calories and spikes blood sugar. When people stop eating these refined products, they often feel better, which makes them think wheat or gluten was the problem, when it may simply have been the fact that their diets were full of unwholesome and unhealthy foods.

Opting for whole wheat flour is a wise decision, but only if the whole wheat is fresh. The polyunsaturated oil in whole wheat is very healthy in its unprocessed state, but it oxidizes very quickly when wheat is ground into flour. It is not uncommon to buy whole wheat products that are rancid, which pose an even worse health problem than does refined flour, as these rancid items can develop toxic compounds and may be carcinogenic. If you want to enjoy truly healthful wheat, store your fresh grains or freshly ground flour in the refrigerator or freezer, and use these ingredients sooner than later.

SPROUTED WHEAT BREAD

This bread is dense, but still tender and moist. It is high in fiber and has a subtle sweetness from the sprouted wheat. The inclusion of vital wheat gluten in the recipe gives it a boost of protein and holds it together. This bread is wonderful when toasted and eaten with your choice of nut butter.

Yield: 1 Loaf

2 cups soft wheat berries	1 package active dry yeast
3 tablespoons rolled oats	$1/_2$ cup vital wheat gluten
1 cup carrot pulp	

1. In a large bowl, cover the wheat berries with water by a few inches. Cover the bowl with a towel and let the grains soak for 10 to 12 hours. Drain the wheat berries in a strainer, rinse them well, and return them to the bowl without water. Cover them again with a towel and let them sit at room temperature, rinsing them twice a day, until $1/_4$-inch white sprouts appear. Depending on the temperature of the room, this process usually takes 1 to 2 days.

2. Preheat the oven to 350°F. Grease an $8^1/_2$-x-$4^1/_2$-inch loaf pan with coconut oil and sprinkle it with the rolled oats. Set aside.

3. In a food processor or Vitamix, combine the sprouted wheat berries, carrot pulp, and yeast. Process until dough forms, using a spatula to scrape the sides of the food processor as needed. (This may take up to 5 minutes, so be patient.)

4. In a large mixing bowl, combine the dough and vital wheat gluten. Knead the dough for about 5 minutes.

5. Place the dough in the prepared loaf pan. Let it rise in a warm (not hot) place for 1 to 2 hours, or until it has almost doubled in size. (Please note that it will not rise as high as a loaf of regular bread.)

6. Bake the loaf for 45 minutes. Carefully remove the loaf from the loaf pan, loosening it around the sides with a butter knife if necessary, and place it upside down on a baking sheet. Bake the loaf for another 15 minutes, or until it is dry and lightly browned on the bottom (which should now be facing up). Allow the loaf to cool on a wire rack before slicing.

CARROT FRUIT ESSENE BREAD

Essene bread has been attributed to a Jewish sect that lived from the second century BC until the first century AD. The sprouted grains in this recipe make it one of the healthiest breads you can eat. It has a thick crust and is very moist, densely chewy, and naturally sweet.

Yield: 6 Rounds

2 cups soft wheat berries, spelt berries, or kamut berries

1/2 **cup carrot pulp**

1 cup raisins or other coarsely chopped dried fruit

1 teaspoon cinnamon

1. In a large bowl, cover the wheat berries with water by a few inches. Cover the bowl with a towel and let the grains soak for 10 to 12 hours. Drain the wheat berries in a strainer, rinse them well, and return them to the bowl without adding more water. Cover them again with a towel and let them sit at room temperature, rinsing them twice a day, until 1/4-inch white sprouts appear. Depending on the temperature of the room, this process usually takes 1 to 2 days after the initial soaking.

2. Preheat the oven to 250°F. Grease an 18-x-13-inch baking sheet with coconut oil and sprinkle it lightly with cornmeal or rolled oats. Set aside.

3. In a food processor, combine the sprouted grains and carrot pulp. Process until dough forms, using a spatula to scrape the sides of the food processor as needed. (This may take up to 5 minutes, so be patient.)

4. Add the raisins and cinnamon to the food processor. Process the dough thoroughly and transfer it to a large mixing bowl.

5. Knead the dough and shape it into 6 flat rounds of equal size. Place the rounds onto the prepared baking sheet. Bake for 2 hours, or until the rounds have a thick crust.

Helpful Tip

If you want the crust to be less chewy, wrap the rounds in a clean towel and place them in a plastic bag while still warm. Remove the towel once they have cooled.

For a Change . . .

To make even more authentic Essene bread, dehydrate the rounds for about 10 hours instead of baking them.

ALMOND PIE CRUST

This is a raw crust for raw pies, or for pies that do not have to be baked after they are filled. It is a crust that anyone can make because all you have to do is grind up the ingredients and press them into a pie pan.

Yield: One 9-Inch Crust

1 cup almonds $1/4$ teaspoon salt

$1/2$ cup soft pitted dates

1. In a food processor, combine the almonds, dates, and salt. Process until coarsely ground.

2. Carefully press the mixture into a 9-inch pie pan. Use immediately, or store in a plastic bag in the refrigerator for 2 to 3 days, or in the freezer for up to 2 weeks.

GLUTEN-FREE SAVORY PIE CRUST

Since so many people are opting for gluten-free foods these days, I decided to create a gluten-free pie crust. This one is tender but crisp, and slices remarkably well. Even if you aren't in need of a gluten-free crust, you may still enjoy this one just for the taste.

Yield: One 9-Inch Crust

1 cup sorghum flour	Pinch of salt
$1/4$ cup garbanzo flour	$1/3$ cup olive oil
1 tablespoon arrowroot powder	$1/4$ cup hot water (heated but not boiling)

1. In a medium-sized mixing bowl, combine the sorghum flour, garbanzo flour, arrowroot powder, and salt.

2. In a small mixing bowl, combine the olive oil and water, but do not mix. Slowly pour the oil and water over the flour mixture, mixing with a fork as you pour. Mix well until dough forms.

3. On a work surface lightly sprinkled with water, place the dough between two sheets of waxed paper. Roll it out to a 12-inch circle.

4. Carefully peel off and discard the top sheet of waxed paper. Pick up the dough by the corners of the bottom sheet of waxed paper and place it paper side up in a 9-inch pie pan. Carefully peel off the waxed paper and gently press the dough into the pan. Flute the edges of the crust. Sprinkle the crust with a pinch more arrowroot powder, distributing it evenly. Use immediately.

Helpful Tip

This dough tears more easily than a wheat dough as it goes into the pan, but you can patch it, if necessary, by transferring excess pieces from the edges to where they are needed, pressing in the patches firmly.

GLUTEN-FREE SWEET PIE CRUST

This pie crust has a nearly identical list of ingredients as its savory version, save for the oil. Since this recipe is meant for sweet pies, coconut oil takes the place of olive oil. It remains a great gluten-free crust that slices easily and tastes wonderful.

Yield: One 9-Inch Crust

1 cup sorghum flour	Pinch of salt
$1/4$ cup garbanzo flour	$1/3$ cup coconut oil
1 tablespoon arrowroot powder	$1/4$ cup hot water (heated but not boiling)

1. In a medium-sized mixing bowl, combine the sorghum flour, garbanzo flour, arrowroot powder, and salt.

2. In a small mixing bowl, combine the coconut oil and water, but do not mix. Slowly pour the oil and water over the flour mixture, mixing with a fork as you pour. Mix well until dough forms.

3. On a work surface lightly sprinkled with water, place the dough between two sheets of waxed paper. Roll it out to a 12-inch circle.

4. Carefully peel off and discard the top sheet of waxed paper. Pick up the dough by the corners of the bottom sheet of waxed paper and place it paper side up in a 9-inch pie pan. Carefully peel off the waxed paper and gently press the dough into the pan. Flute the edges of the crust. Sprinkle the crust with a pinch more arrowroot powder, distributing it evenly. Use immediately.

Helpful Tip

This dough tears more easily than a wheat dough as it goes into the pan, but you can patch it, if necessary, by transferring excess pieces from the edges to where they are needed, pressing in the patches firmly.

HOLIDAY CORN CAKES

If you like cornbread stuffing and cranberry sauce, here they are all rolled up into one recipe! When I was growing up in Kentucky, my mother used to fry up cornbread in her cast-iron skillet. These corn cakes are a spiced-up vegan version of my mother's old Southern favorite.

Yield: About 16 Corn Cakes

1 cup fine cornmeal

$1/3$ cup garbanzo flour

$1/2$ teaspoon baking soda

$1/2$ teaspoon baking powder

$1/2$ teaspoon salt

$1/3$ cup frozen sweet corn

$1/2$ cup raisins (optional)

$1/4$ cup finely chopped scallions

2 tablespoons minced fresh sage

$1/4$ cup cranberry juice

$1/2$ cup cranberry pulp

$1 1/2$ cup unsweetened soy milk

Freshly ground black pepper to taste

2 tablespoons olive oil, divided

1. In a large mixing bowl, combine the cornmeal, garbanzo flour, baking soda, baking powder, and salt. Mix well. Add the sweet corn, raisins, scallions, and sage. Mix well.

2. In a medium-sized mixing bowl, combine the cranberry juice, cranberry pulp, soy milk, and black pepper. Mix well. Add the wet ingredients to the dry ingredients. Mix well.

3. In a 12-inch skillet, heat the olive oil over medium-high heat. Add four $1/4$-cup portions of batter to the skillet. Cook until each cake is brown on the bottom. Flip the cakes over and continue to cook until crispy brown. Add the remaining batter in $1/4$-cup portions and cook as directed in step 3 until all the batter has been used.

4

Comfortably Enjoy the Salads . . . and Soups

If you juice, you have an extraordinary culinary tool at your fingertips. The soup recipes in this chapter take advantage of both pulp and juice. You can make a good soup recipe even better by replacing some of the broth or water with fresh juice. Because it is so colorful, flavorful, and nutritious, fresh juice can enhance any soup to which it is added. Pulp is usually best added to soups that will be blended into a creamy texture, so it essentially disappears. Then again, some recipes, such as Borscht (page 62) and Cold Cucumber Cream Soup (page 58), blend only a portion of the soup and are still wonderful. Pulp-based broth is a frugal and healthy way to bring flavor and nutrients to any soup you like, and it can also make use of any stringy or tough pulp that is not good to use directly in a dish.

If you are not a fan of cold soups, please make an exception and try any of the ones in this chapter. On a hot summer's day, they are so deliciously refreshing. I especially love gazpacho. Of course, the hot soups found in this chapter are fantastic, too, and are sure to satisfy the more conventional eaters seated at your dinner table. There is something here for everyone.

Some hardcore juicing enthusiasts simply toss pulp with a little salad dressing and eat it as a proper salad. I, on the other hand, cannot go quite so far. Nevertheless, it is true that certain types of pulp don't need a whole lot of extra ingredients to become tasty enough to enjoy. I think one of the tricks to using pulp in salads is to use it conservatively. More is not necessarily better.

The salads in this chapter are sure to amaze you. They are often a delight both to eat and to see. Land and Sea Salad (page 71) is a super nutritious dish that can be served for a light lunch, Carrot and Pineapple Salad (page 70) is deceptively simple and tasty, and Autumn Salad (page 69) is sure to please with its lovely combination of flavors.

COLD CUCUMBER CREAM SOUP

When your guests try this soup, they will think you used cream to make it. When you tell them you didn't, don't be surprised if they don't believe you. When making a cold soup such as this one, use produce straight out of the refrigerator. Doing so will allow you to serve the soup immediately without chilling it.

Yield: 4 Servings

2 cups cucumber juice	2 tablespoons white or yellow miso
³/₄ cup cucumber pulp	
1 cup celery juice	3 tablespoons lemon juice
12.3 ounces extra-firm silken tofu	2 to 3 scallions, finely chopped
	2 tablespoons finely chopped fresh dill

1. In a large mixing bowl, combine the cucumber juice and cucumber pulp.

2. In a blender, combine the celery juice, tofu, and miso. Blend until creamy. Add the mixture to the large bowl. Mix well.

3. Add the lemon juice, scallions, and dill to the large mixing bowl. Stir well and serve immediately, or cover and chill in the refrigerator until ready to serve.

MELON-MINT SOUP

I once had a Cavaillon melon—a scrumptious regional delicacy from Provence—although the waiter called it "melon de Cavaillon," of course. It was served halved and garnished with mint leaves. This simple melon soup was inspired by that meal and makes a delicious starter to an elegant summer dinner.

Yield: 4 Servings

$1/2$ cup fresh mint leaves, packed

1 small honeydew melon or cantaloupe, peeled and cut into wedges

1. Juice the mint leaves and honeydew melon together.

2. In a medium-sized mixing bowl, combine the juice and juicing pulp. Stir well, cover, and chill in the refrigerator until ready to serve.

For a Change . . .

This recipe may also be adjusted to make a fabulous sorbet. (See page 129.)

The Little Differences

To make fabulous green juices that are not too bitter or too sweet, use lots of cucumber, romaine lettuce, fennel, or celery. Add enough apple and lemon to make it delicious, and go light on strong greens such as kale, parsley, and dandelion.

MANGO-CUCUMBER SOUP

This cooling and delicious soup can be spiced up or toned down to suit your taste. I've even had leftovers of this dish for breakfast, though without the onion or chipotle.

Yield: 4 Servings

3 medium-sized mangoes, peeled, pitted, and cut into wedges

1 lime, peeled

1-inch piece ginger

1 large cucumber

1 cup coconut milk

$1/2$ teaspoon ground coriander

$1/2$ cup finely chopped fresh cilantro

1. Juice the mangoes. Transfer the juice and pulp to a large mixing bowl.

2. Juice the lime, ginger, and cucumber. Add the juice to the large mixing bowl.

3. Add the coconut milk and coriander to the large mixing bowl. Stir well, cover, and chill in the refrigerator until ready to serve. Top the soup with the cilantro before serving.

For a Change . . .

If you are a feeling adventurous, add $1/3$ cup minced sweet onion and $1/2$ teaspoon ground chipotle. For a pretty presentation, add a few drops of coconut milk to each bowl before serving, letting the drops float on top of the soup.

MY FAVORITE GAZPACHO

I love the way the carrot juice mellows out the acidity of the tomatoes in this recipe. I recommend chilling all the ingredients until you are ready to make the soup and serving it as soon as it is ready.

Yield: 6 Servings

3 cups tomato juice	$1/2$ bell pepper, minced
1 cup tomato pulp	2 scallions, finely chopped
2 cups carrot juice	1 clove garlic, pressed
$1/2$ lemon, unpeeled, seeded, and juiced	2 tablespoons minced fresh basil
1 cucumber, grated	$1/4$ teaspoon salt, or to taste

1. In a large mixing bowl, combine the tomato juice, tomato pulp, carrot juice, and lemon juice.

2. Add the cucumber, bell pepper, scallions, garlic, basil, and salt to the large mixing bowl. Stir well. Serve immediately, or cover and chill in the refrigerator until ready to serve.

Helpful Tip

Leftovers may be stored in a covered container in the refrigerator for a day or two, but this dish is best freshly made.

Best Intentions

Keep your juicer out on the counter. It is the only way you will use it, regardless of your best intentions.

BORSCHT

This simple borscht with its lovely pink topping looks as good as it tastes.

Yield: 6 to 8 Servings

$1^1/_2$ pounds potatoes, scrubbed and diced

1 cup beet pulp

$^1/_2$ cup carrot pulp

1 cup finely chopped onion

4 bay leaves

1 teaspoon tarragon

4 tablespoons tamari

2 tablespoons balsamic vinegar

6 cups water

$^1/_2$ cup beet juice (optional)

CREAMY PINK TOPPING

1 cup raw cashews, soaked for 1 hour and then drained

$^1/_2$ cucumber

$^1/_2$ lemon, peeled

2 cloves garlic

$^1/_4$ teaspoon salt, or to taste

1. In a 6-quart stockpot, combine the potatoes, beet pulp, carrot pulp, onion, bay leaves, tarragon, tamari, balsamic vinegar, and water. Cover and bring to a boil. Reduce the heat and simmer for 20 to 30 minutes, or until the vegetables are tender.

2. Remove a ladle or two of the soup and transfer to a blender. Blend until creamy. Mix the blended portion into the stockpot.

3. To prepare the topping, juice the cucumber and lemon together.

4. In a blender, combine $^1/_2$ cup cucumber and lemon juice, cashews, garlic, and salt. Blend until very smooth and creamy. Transfer the topping to a small bowl and set aside.

5. Once the soup is completely cooked, add the beet juice to the stockpot. Stir well. Serve hot, or cover and chill in the refrigerator until ready to serve. Top with a dollop of topping before serving.

Helpful Tip

The topping may be used immediately after it has been made, but it is best chilled, as it thickens in the refrigerator.

PARSLEY-POTATO SOUP

Thanks to the parsley, this soup has a lovely freshness to it, while being hearty and satisfying at the same time. It may also be served warm or chilled like a vichyssoise.

Yield: 6 Servings

2 pounds potatoes, scrubbed and diced

$1^1/_2$ cup finely chopped onion

$1^1/_2$ cups finely chopped celery

3 cups water

2 cups unsweetened soy milk

$^1/_3$ **cup parsley pulp**

$^1/_4$ cup white miso

$^1/_3$ **cup celery pulp (optional)**

$^1/_3$ cup parsley juice (optional)

$^1/_2$ teaspoon white pepper, or to taste

1. In a 6-quart stockpot, combine the potatoes, onion, celery, and water. Cover and bring to a boil. Reduce the heat to simmer and cook for about 30 minutes, or until the vegetables are tender. Remove the stockpot from the heat.

2. In a blender, combine the milk, parsley pulp, miso, celery pulp, parsley juice, and one ladleful of vegetables from the stockpot. Blend until smooth.

3. In the stockpot, combine the blended mixture and cooked vegetables. Stir well. Season with the white pepper and serve immediately.

For a Change . . .

To try this soup cold, blend the entire soup, cover, and chill in the refrigerator before serving. A handful of cashews added to the blender will give the soup a creamy texture. You may also use spinach juice or spinach pulp instead of parsley.

SUMMER SQUASH SOUP

In this recipe, the juicer creates a purée, so you won't have any need for a blender. If your juicer is already sitting on your kitchen counter, this soup will prove a quick and simple dinner when you are short on time. I love it with homemade whole grain croutons soaking in it!

Yield: 6 Servings

1 tablespoon olive oil

$1^1/_4$ cup finely chopped onion

2 lbs summer squash (zucchini, yellow squash, or patty pan), peeled and juiced

$^1/_2$ cup finely chopped parsley

2 cups unsweetened soy milk

$^1/_4$ cup minced fresh basil, or 1 teaspoon dried basil

$^1/_2$ teaspoon white pepper

3 tablespoons yellow miso, or to taste

1. In a 6-quart stockpot, heat the olive oil over medium heat. Add the onion and sauté for about 5 minutes, or until tender and lightly browned.

2. Add the squash juice, squash pulp, and parsley to the stockpot. Cover and cook for about 10 minutes, stirring occasionally.

3. Add the milk, basil, and white pepper to the stockpot. Reduce the heat to simmer. In a measuring cup, combine $^1/_2$ cup soup with the miso. Stir well to dissolve the miso. Take the soup off the heat. Add the miso mixture to the stockpot. Stir well and serve immediately.

Helpful Tip

To reheat any soup that contains miso while also preserving its probiotic properties, heat the soup in a saucepan over medium-high heat until warm, stirring regularly. Do not bring it to a boil.

SOUTHWEST TOMATO SOUP

When tomatoes are in season, it is time to make this soup. The beans, corn, rice, and cooked vegetables make it hearty, but the raw tomato juice keeps it light and fresh.

Yield: 6 Servings

2 tablespoons olive oil	1 cup cooked brown rice
1$^1/_2$ cups finely chopped onion	1 cup corn
1 or 2 stalks celery, finely chopped	$^1/_4$ cup finely chopped fresh basil
	1 teaspoon cumin
1 bell pepper, diced	$^1/_4$ teaspoon chipotle, or to taste
1 yellow squash, diced	2 tablespoons tamari
1$^1/_4$ cups tomato pulp	1 tablespoon balsamic vinegar
1$^1/_2$ cups cooked black beans	3$^1/_2$ cups tomato juice

1. In a 6-quart stockpot, heat the olive oil over medium heat. Add the onion and celery. Sauté until the onion becomes translucent. Add the bell pepper, squash, and tomato pulp. Reduce the heat to low. Cover and cook for about 15 to 20 minutes, or until the vegetables are tender.

2. Add the black beans, brown rice, corn, basil, cumin, and chipotle to the stockpot. Simmer for 5 minutes. Add the tamari and balsamic vinegar. Simmer for another minute.

3. Add the tomato juice to the stockpot. Heat through but do not boil. Stir well and serve immediately.

For a Change...

Try using diced butternut squash instead of yellow squash and leaving out the brown rice.

CARROT SPICE SOUP

The subtle flavors of sweet and savory spices give this soup an Indian flair. If it is not too much of a culture clash for you, try this soup with cornbread for a light, easy, and out-of-the-ordinary meal.

Yield: 6 to 8 Servings

2 tablespoons olive oil

2 cups finely chopped onion

2 cups finely chopped celery

1 teaspoon turmeric

$1/2$ teaspoon cinnamon

$1/2$ teaspoon allspice

$1/2$ teaspoon nutmeg

4 cups water

$1^1/_2$ pounds potatoes, diced

$1^1/_2$ cup carrot pulp

$1^1/_2$ teaspoons salt

1 cup unsweetened soy milk or other unsweetened nondairy milk

1 cup carrot juice

Pinch of cayenne

1. In a 12-inch skillet, heat the olive oil over medium heat. Add the onion and celery. Sauté until the onion is just beginning to get tender. Add the turmeric, cinnamon, allspice, and nutmeg. Stir, cover, reduce the heat to low, and cook for about 10 minutes, or until the onion and celery are tender.

2. In a 6-quart stockpot, combine the water, potatoes, carrot pulp, and salt. Cover, bring to a boil, reduce the heat to simmer for about 20 minutes, or until the potatoes tender. Transfer to a blender and blend until smooth and creamy.

3. Pour the blended mixture back into the stockpot and add the sautéed onion and celery. Stir, bring to a boil, and reduce the heat to simmer. Stir in the milk. Turn off the heat and stir in the juice. Stir in the cayenne and serve immediately.

For a Change . . .

Substitute tarragon, thyme, or herbes de Provence for the turmeric, cinnamon, allspice, and nutmeg spices, and substitute white pepper for the cayenne.

FRESH BROTH

Preparing this broth is so easy that you don't really need a recipe, but I will give you one anyway. You may use just about any kind of vegetable pulp—kale, parsley, celery, or any type of greens is great for this recipe, as is carrot or tomato. Avoid beet or red cabbage pulp, though, unless you would like a red broth. You can throw green onion tops, potato peels, or the wilted outside leaves of salad greens into the pot as well, and if you mix in a little garlic or ginger, the broth gets even better.

Yield: About 7 Cups

2 cups vegetable pulp

8 cups water

4 bay leaves

2 teaspoons herbes de Provence or your own choice of dried herbs

Salt or tamari to taste

1. In a 6-quart stockpot, combine the vegetable pulp, water, bay leaves, and herbes de Provence. Cover and bring to a boil. Reduce the heat and simmer for about 30 minutes.

2. Using a fine wire strainer, strain the broth into a large bowl. Add the salt. Use the broth immediately to make soup, or freeze it for later use.

VEGETABLE BROTH POWDER

It is easy to make your own homemade veggie broth powder to use in soups and sauces. As mentioned in the Fresh Broth recipe (page 67), you can use kale, parsley, celery, carrots, tomatoes, garlic, ginger, or any type of greens to make this broth powder.

Yield: About 1 Cup

2 cups vegetable pulp	1 teaspoon salt
$1/4$ cup dried onion flakes	1 teaspoon turmeric
$1/4$ cup nutritional yeast	2 teaspoons dried basil

1. Place the vegetable pulp in a dehydrator and dehydrate at 120°F for 10 hours, or until completely dry and brittle.

2. In a blender or food processor, combine the dehydrated pulp and onion flakes. Grind into a fine powder.

3. In a medium-sized mixing bowl, combine the ground pulp, nutritional yeast, salt, turmeric, and basil. Mix well.

4. Place the vegetable broth powder in an airtight container and store it in the cupboard. It should last for a few months if properly dried, but if you notice mold, it was not completely dried when stored and must be discarded.

Helpful Tip

To make broth, stir 1 heaping teaspoon vegetable broth powder into 1 cup boiling water. If you want clear broth without any pulp, strain it through a coffee strainer after allowing it to sit for about 5 minutes. To make the broth powder even more flavorful, before you dehydrate the vegetable pulp, add $1/2$ cup vegetable juice.

AUTUMN SALAD

This recipe came to me after I'd drunk a surprisingly delicious glass of red cabbage and pink lady apple juice. The French say we eat first with our eyes, and this richly colored salad certainly makes that statement true.

Yield: 6 Servings

1 cup shredded red cabbage

$1/_2$ cup cabbage pulp

$1/_2$ cup apple pulp

1 cup finely chopped curly endive

$1/_2$ cup halved red grapes

$1/_3$ cup coarsely chopped pecans

$1/_3$ cup raisins

1 apple, diced

$1/_4$ cup lime juice or apple cider vinegar

2 tablespoons olive oil

2 teaspoons fresh tarragon, or $1/_2$ teaspoon dried

1 teaspoon dill seed

$1/_2$ teaspoon salt

Freshly ground black pepper to taste

1. In a large salad bowl, combine the red cabbage, cabbage pulp, apple pulp, curly endive, grapes, pecans, raisins, apple, lime juice, olive oil, tarragon, dill seed, salt, and pepper. Toss well.

2. Serve immediately, or refrigerate and serve chilled.

Helpful Tip

Curly endive is quite coarse but so good for you. If you chop it finely, it is delicious, and you can enjoy it in large quantities.

For a Change . . .

Instead of the grapes, use orange pieces and a bit of orange zest for a tangy flavor.

CARROT AND PINEAPPLE SALAD

This salad is so simple that I am always surprised by how good it is. It is wonderful on its own or as a colorful side for a bean or grain dish.

Yield: 4 Servings

1 cup carrot pulp

$1/2$ cup pineapple pulp

$1/4$ cup pineapple juice

2 or 3 stalks celery, finely chopped

$1/4$ cup coarsely chopped pecans or walnuts

1. In a large salad bowl, combine the carrot pulp, pineapple pulp, pineapple juice, celery, and pecans. Toss well.

2. Serve immediately, or refrigerate and serve chilled.

Helpful Tip

If this salad is too pulpy for you, toss in some grated carrot and chunks of pineapple. If you'd like a sweeter salad, add a handful of raisins.

The Difference is Huge

Very fibrous pulp, such as celery pulp or kale pulp, is best used in broth preparation because it simply doesn't work well in other recipes. Reasonable amounts of this type of pulp, however, may be used in recipes when mixed with carrot, beet, spinach, or cabbage pulp—just pick out the stringy parts. It may also be blended into soups or smoothies.

LAND AND SEA SALAD

The dulse gives this recipe a mild seafood taste as well as beneficial minerals. Although it's been decades since I have had tuna salad, the color, texture, and flavor of this dish remind me of that classic meal.

Yield: 3 to 4 Servings

$1/_2$ cup cabbage pulp

$1/_2$ cup carrot pulp

$1/_2$ cup cucumber pulp

$1/_3$ cup finely chopped celery

$1/_3$ cup dulse flakes

$1/_4$ cup minced sweet onion

$1/_4$ cup mayonnaise

2 tablespoons freshly grated horseradish, or 1 tablespoon prepared horseradish

1 tablespoon lime juice

$1/_4$ teaspoon celery seeds

1. In a large salad bowl, combine the cabbage pulp, carrot pulp, cucumber pulp, celery, dulse flakes, sweet onion, mayonnaise, horseradish, lime juice, and celery seeds. Toss well.

2. Serve immediately on toast or a bed of lettuce, or refrigerate and serve chilled.

Helpful Tip

To make this dish vegan, use vegan mayonnaise, which may be purchased at any health food store.

Pretty Smart

Cucumber is known among juicing enthusiasts as being good for your skin. Use cucumber pulp in a beauty mask combined with some mashed avocado. Leave it on your face for about 30 minutes, and your skin will look and feel fabulous.

GREEN SLAW
WITH AVOCADO DRESSING

The avocado dressing makes this slaw healthier, prettier, and tastier than almost any slaw you can find, and it's a great way to use cabbage, a nutritious and underused vegetable.

Yield: 6 Servings

$1^1/_2$ cups shredded cabbage

1 cup shredded carrot

1 cup cabbage pulp or carrot pulp

1 small avocado, diced

2 scallions, finely chopped

1 recipe Avocado Dressing (page 76)

1. In a large salad bowl, combine the cabbage, carrot, cabbage pulp, avocado, and scallions. Toss well.

2. Pour most of the dressing over the salad, reserving enough to garnish each serving with a small dollop. Toss well and serve immediately.

Helpful Tip

For aesthetic reasons, it is best not to mix the two types of pulp in this recipe.

Best Intentions

Everyone loves the rush of nutrition that comes from a shot of fresh juice, but don't forget to eat proper meals. Juice is a wonderful supplement to a balanced diet, not a replacement.

TEMPEH SALAD WITH TAHINI DRESSING

This hearty and delicious salad becomes a satisfying meal when served on a bed of salad greens and accompanied by a slice or two of whole grain bread. It is also great as sandwich filling or as stuffing for lettuce rolls.

Yield: 3 to 4 Servings

8-ounce package tempeh, cubed

1 cup frozen peas

1 cup carrot pulp

$1/2$ cup minced celery

$1/2$ cup quartered cherry or grape tomatoes

$1/4$ cup finely chopped scallions

$1/4$ cup fresh basil chiffonade

1 heaping tablespoon capers

1 recipe Tahini Dressing (page 76)

1. Steam the tempeh for about 15 minutes, and then add the frozen peas to the steamer. Steam the peas for about 1 minute to thaw.

2. In a large salad bowl, combine the steamed tempeh and peas, carrot pulp, celery, cherry tomatoes, scallions, basil, and capers.

3. Pour most of the dressing over the salad, reserving enough to garnish each serving with a small dollop. Toss well and serve immedaitely.

Helpful Tip

I once poured about $1/3$ cup carrot juice on leftovers of this salad. The leftovers soaked up the juice and the whole thing was delicious! As such, though, it would be too wet to use as sandwich filling.

JUICER SAUERKRAUT

This recipe was inspired by the method my mother taught me to make sauerkraut, which is the easiest I have ever found. I have made it tastier and easier by using cabbage pulp and juice rather than chopped or shredded cabbage and water.

Yield: Four 32-ounce Canning Jars

1 large very fresh cabbage   4 teaspoons salt

1. Remove the tough outer leaves of the cabbage. Juice the cabbage.

2. In a large mixing bowl, combine the cabbage juice and cabbage pulp. Mix well.

3. Add $1/2$ teaspoon salt to the bottom of 1 canning jar. Fill the jar with the cabbage juice and pulp mixture, packing it well. Leave $3/4$-inch space at the top of the jar. Sprinkle another $1/2$ teaspoon salt on top.

4. Repeat step 3 and with the remaining mixture.

5. Place the lids on the jars and secure them. Store the jars in a dark place at room temperature until fermented, which should take about 4 days, but may take longer. When the sauerkraut is as sour as you would like, store the jars in the refrigerator for three to four months.

Helpful Tip

You will need very clean canning jars with new lids. Just to be safe, I always boil the jars in water for 10 minutes before filling them. I also dip the lids in boiling water before placing them on the jars. The amount of time for fermentation depends on temperature. When I lived in Canada, the process took much longer than it does in Florida, which takes only 3 to 4 days.

Be careful not to fill the jars too much—if you do, the liquid will spew out as it ferments, making a mess. In fact, it may be a good idea to place the jars on a towel or tray during the fermentation process, just in case.

For a Change . . .

Add dill seed or caraway seed to the sauerkraut.

KEY LIME CHOPPED SALAD

The pulp in this salad enhances its flavor by soaking up the lime juice and distributing it evenly throughout. When combined, these ingredients create a very tasty dish that doesn't even require salt or oil.

Yield: 4 to 6 Servings

1 cup carrot pulp

1 cup diced cucumber

1 cup quartered cherry or grape tomatoes

1 cup diced avocado

$^1/_4$ cup finely chopped scallions

2 tablespoons key lime juice

2 to 3 tablespoons fresh basil chiffonade

1. In a large salad bowl, combine the carrot pulp, cucumber, cherry tomatoes, avocado, scallions, key lime juice, and basil. Toss well.

2. Serve immediately, or refrigerate and serve chilled.

Helpful Tip

You can substitute regular lime juice or even lemon juice for the key lime juice. You could also add a little garlic if you'd like.

AVOCADO DRESSING

Creamy avocado delectably hides pulp. Lime juice and cucumber juice add nutrients and keep the dressing a beautiful bright green, which is a great improvement on typical avocado dressings.

Yield: About 1$^1/_2$ Cups

1 medium avocado	$^1/_2$ **cup cucumber pulp**
1 clove garlic	2 tablespoons parsley juice (optional)
$^1/_4$ cup lime juice	
$^1/_2$ cup cucumber juice	Pinch of salt

1. In a blender, combine the avocado, garlic, lime juice, cucumber juice, cucumber pulp, parsley juice, and salt. Blend until creamy, using a spatula to scrape the sides of the blender as needed.

2. Use immediately, or store in a covered container in the refrigerator for up to 1 week.

TAHINI DRESSING

Made with water, this is a lot like a classic tahini dressing, but made with carrot juice this dressing turns a rich caramel color and has a hint of sweetness. Use it on Tempeh Salad (page 73) or a green salad.

Yield: About $^3/_4$ Cup

$^1/_3$ cup tahini	1 clove garlic, pressed
$^1/_4$ cup carrot juice or water	2 tablespoons balsamic vinegar
2 tablespoons tamari	

1. In a small mixing bowl, combine the tahini, carrot juice, tamari, garlic, and balsamic vinegar. Stir well to achieve a smooth consistency.

2. Use immediately, or store in a covered container in the refrigerator for up to 1 week.

PEACH TARRAGON DRESSING

This dressing is especially delicious when made with flax oil, but olive oil would be good, too. Try it over baby spinach or arugula topped with chopped walnuts for a salad that is both simple and elegant.

Yield: About 1¹/₄ Cups

$^1/_4$ cup peach juice

$^1/_2$ cup peach pulp

$^1/_4$ cup flax oil

2 tablespoons apple cider vinegar

1 heaping tablespoon finely chopped onion

1 tablespoon coarsely chopped fresh tarragon, or 1 teaspoon dried

$^1/_2$ teaspoon salt

1. In a blender, combine the peach juice, peach pulp, flax oil, apple cider vinegar, onion, tarragon, and salt. Blend until creamy, using a spatula to scrape the sides of the blender as needed.

2. Use immediately, or store in a covered container in the refrigerator for up to 1 week.

Correctamundo

Your nose knows! There's a lot of rancid oil out there. You can find it in nuts, grains, baked products, and snack foods. It tastes bad and is bad for you, so when you open any product that contains oil, nuts, or whole grains, give it a sniff. If it smells rancid, then take it back to the store and trade it in for something fresh.

TOMATO BASIL DRESSING

This flavorful tomato pulp dressing is so good that all you need is a simple bed of tender young lettuce to go with it for a great salad.

Yield: About 1 Cup

$1/4$ cup tomato juice

$1/2$ cup tomato pulp

1 clove garlic

$1/4$ cup olive oil

2 tablespoons balsamic vinegar

1 teaspoon dried basil

$1/2$ teaspoon sea salt

1. In a blender, combine the tomato juice, tomato pulp, garlic, olive oil, balsamic vinegar, basil, and sea salt. Blend until creamy, using a spatula to scrape the sides of the blender as needed.

2. Use immediately, or store in a covered container in the refrigerator for up to 1 week.

For a Change . . .

By adding 1 tablespoon maple syrup or a few drops of Stevia, this dressing will taste like a fresh version of the bottled French dressing that was likely on your childhood dinner table. I prefer it without the added sweetness, but if you ever get nostalgic . . .

Helpful Tip

Olive oil will typically congeal in the refrigerator. To allow the congealed olive oil to liquefy, remove the container of dressing from the refrigerator and bring it to room temperature before using.

5

Bring Out the Dips...
and Sauces and Spreads

With a little creativity, pulp can be the base of many delicious spreads, sauces, salsas, or dips. For sauces, use pulp that is naturally wet and saucy, like tomato, spinach, or fruit pulp. Tomato pulp is especially versatile, as you will see in Almost Instant Tomato Sauce (page 81) and Tomato Curry Sauce (page 80). Fruit pulp is the perfect starter for sweet sauces to use over pancakes, oatmeal, or your choice of dessert.

Carrot pulp and other types of pulp with a dryer texture can be used in spreads and dips. Using pulp in a spread or dip is also easy to do. While a couple of the recipes in this chapter are baked (including one of my favorites, Shiitake Pâté, on page 91), for most of the spreads and dips, all that is required is a bit of blending or mixing—no oven needed.

Add a few spices and almost any type of pulp can be used to make chutney, as long as the pulp isn't too tough or stringy. This chapter's Coconut Chutney (page 86) and Pineapple Chutney (page 87) are great examples of how the right spices can enliven pulp and result in a sauce or dip that transforms even the most plain bean and rice dish into a great meal.

Hopefully these recipes for sauces, spreads, and dips will encourage you to experiment with different combinations of grains, beans, and veggies, and help you see an endless number of culinary opportunities at your fingertips. Let them open the door to variety in your daily meals.

TOMATO CURRY SAUCE

Your whole house will smell like an Indian restaurant when you make this amazing sauce. Use it as a base for many different curry dishes, from dal to vegetables.

Yield: About 1¹/₂ Cups

3 cloves garlic, peeled

1¹/₂-inch piece ginger, peeled and sliced

1 medium-sized onion, quartered

5 medium-sized roma tomatoes, halved

2 tablespoons olive oil

¹/₂ teaspoon mustard seeds

¹/₂ teaspoon onion seeds

¹/₃ cup packed fresh curry leaves (optional)

1 teaspoon ground cumin

¹/₂ teaspoon turmeric

¹/₂ teaspoon ground cardamom

¹/₄ teaspoon cinnamon

¹/₂ teaspoon salt, or to taste

Pinch of cayenne pepper (optional)

1. Juice the garlic, ginger, onion, and tomatoes. Reserve the juice and pulp.

2. In a 2¹/₂-quart saucepan, heat the olive oil over medium-low heat. Add the mustard seeds and onion seeds. Sauté until they begin to pop. Remove the saucepan from the heat and add the curry leaves. Return the pan to the heat and sauté for 1 or 2 minutes.

3. Add the reserved juice, reserved pulp, cumin, turmeric, cardamom, cinnamon, and salt to the saucepan. Simmer uncovered for about 10 minutes, or until the sauce is reduced to the desired consistency.

4. Add the cayenne pepper and stir. Add more salt if desired.

Helpful Tip

If you don't want to deal with the long list of spices, simply use 1 tablespoon curry powder instead. Curry leaves may be purchased in stores that sell Indian foods, but if you don't have access to such groceries, just omit the leaves. Don't bother using dried leaves, as they are not very flavorful.

ALMOST INSTANT TOMATO SAUCE

This isn't your grandmother's slowly simmered tomato sauce. This light and tasty sauce comes together very quickly. If you juice during tomato season, be sure to juice some tomatoes. This sauce is good over veggie burgers, pasta dishes, or any bean or grain dish.

Yield: About 2$^1/_2$ Cups

2 cups roma tomato juice	$^1/_2$ teaspoon sea salt
$^1/_2$ cup roma tomato pulp	1 clove garlic, peeled (optional)
1$^1/_2$ tablespoons arrowroot	Pinch of ground cloves (optional)
$^1/_4$ cup chopped fresh basil	Freshly ground black pepper to taste (optional)

1. In a 2$^1/_2$-quart saucepan, combine the tomato juice and tomato pulp over medium-high heat.

2. Whisk the arrowroot into the saucepan until dissolved. Add the basil, salt, garlic, and ground cloves. Bring to a boil while stirring. The sauce will immediately thicken. Add the black pepper and stir.

FUCHSIA VELOUTÉ SAUCE

The velvety texture and surprising color of this sauce is sure to delight your guests. Try it over a mixture of steamed vegetables or cooked grains for a picture perfect dish.

Yield: About 1$^1/_2$ Cups

1 cup water	$^1/_4$ teaspoon salt
$^1/_3$ cup beet juice	$^1/_8$ teaspoon nutmeg
$^1/_2$ cup beet pulp	$^1/_2$ teaspoon shawarma spice blend (optional)
$^1/_3$ cup cashew pieces	

1. In a blender, combine the water, beet juice, beet pulp, cashew pieces, salt, nutmeg, and shawarma spice blend. Blend for 1 to 2 minutes, or until smooth.

2. Transfer the mixture to a 2$^1/_2$-quart saucepan over high heat. Whisk the mixture until it comes to a boil and thickens.

Helpful Tip

Shawarma spice blend is generally available at grocery stores that sell foods from the Middle East.

For a Change . . .

For a different taste sensation, omit the shawarma spice blend and serve over Green Mashed Potatoes (page 108).

QUICK MUSHROOM SAUCE

Sauces don't have to be high in fat or unhealthy to be good. This quick sauce will enhance a variety of dishes with flavor and nutrients. It can be made with a mixture of juice and water, or simply with the liquid leftover from cooking vegetables. Try it over veggie burgers or loaves, grain dishes, tofu or tempeh dishes, or steamed vegetables.

Yield: About 2^1/$_2$ Cups

2 cups sliced mushrooms	3 tablespoons arrowroot powder
1 cup cold water	2 tablespoons tamari
1 cup carrot juice	1 teaspoon toasted sesame oil

1. In a 1^1/$_2$-quart saucepan, combine the mushrooms, water, carrot juice, arrowroot powder, tamari, and sesame oil over medium-high heat. Mix well to dissolve the arrowroot powder. Bring to a boil, stirring constantly.

2. Reduce the heat to low and simmer for 1 to 2 minutes, stirring constantly, or until the sauce thickens and the mushrooms are done.

Correctamundo

When cooking and juicing, it is almost impossible to go wrong with fresh local produce grown on organic soil. Without artificial fertilizers, farmers must pay more attention to the quality of the soil, which feeds the plants that feed you. Doing so results in better tasting, more nutritious produce.

RED PEPPER SAUCE

This sauce has a texture similar to mayonnaise, as well as a sweet and tangy zip. The bright orange color is striking, making it fun to pair with green vegetables for tasty dish with great visual appeal.

Yield: 1 Cup

2/3 cup cashews

1/2 cup red bell pepper juice

1/3 cup red bell pepper pulp

1 tablespoon yellow miso

1 tablespoon apple cider vinegar

1 clove garlic, peeled

Pinch of cayenne pepper

1. In a blender, combine the cashews, bell pepper juice, bell pepper pulp, miso, apple cider vinegar, garlic, and cayenne pepper. Blend until very creamy. If necessary, add a little water or more juice to the blender.

2. Serve over steamed vegetables such as asparagus, broccoli, or Romanesco. It may also be served as a dip, or even as topping for a baked potato.

The Difference is Huge

Try miso in your pulp dishes. Use it in delicious plant-based creams or tomato-based soups, sauces, salad dressings, or stews. It adds a bold, salty flavor, as well as healthy bacteria. Just make sure not to cook your food after adding miso, as heat destroys its probiotic quality.

PULP SALSA

Better than jarred, this quick salsa may be mixed into beans and rice to liven them up. Of course, it is also great when served as a dip alongside a bowl of tortilla chips.

Yield: About 1$^1/_2$ Cups

1 cup tomato pulp

$^1/_2$ cup finely chopped bell pepper

$^1/_3$ cup finely chopped cilantro

$^1/_4$ cup minced sweet onion

$^1/_2$ to 2 jalapeño peppers, minced

2 tablespoons lime juice

$^1/_4$ teaspoon salt

$^1/_2$ medium-sized tomato, minced

1. If the tomato pulp is too chunky for salsa, blend it quickly in a blender, but stop before it becomes completely smooth. If the pulp is a desirable texture, proceed to step 2.

2. In a medium-sized mixing bowl, combine the tomato pulp, bell pepper, cilantro, sweet onion, jalapeño peppers, lime juice, salt, and tomato. Mix well and serve.

Best Intentions

If you'd like to feel better and look healthier, take the time to learn how to prepare delicious plant-based meals from fresh local ingredients. Invite a few friends over to enjoy these dishes with you and you may just notice your spirit getting lighter as well.

COCONUT CHUTNEY

This chutney goes beautifully with Indian curries. Make it as hot or mild as you'd like. Instead of juice, ripe coconut meat run through a juicer should produce a thick coconut cream.

Yield: About 1 Cup

1/2 cup coconut cream	1/2 teaspoon ground cardamom
1 cup coconut pulp	1/2 teaspoon ground coriander
2 tablespoons minced cilantro	1/8 teaspoon salt
2 tablespoons lime juice	1 chili or jalapeño pepper, minced (optional)

1. In a medium-sized mixing bowl, combine the coconut cream, coconut pulp, cilantro, lime juice, cardamom, coriander, salt, and chili pepper. Mix well.

2. Serve the chutney with a curry dish, or store it in a covered container in the refrigerator for up to 1 week. Allow the chutney to return to room temperature before serving from the refrigerator.

Helpful Tip

I juice coconut meat in my Champion juicer without a problem, as long as I go very slowly and don't try to force it. This will not work in all juicers, though, and may even be too tough on a Champion if you're juicing a lot of coconut meat. As an alternative, you can make wonderful coconut milk instead by chopping the meat of one fresh coconut into 1-inch chunks and blending them in a blender with 2 cups water. Slowly pour this slurry though the hopper of your juicer to make homemade coconut milk without having to strain it though a cloth. The result will be delicious coconut milk and pulp, and the process will have been easier on the juicer.

PINEAPPLE CHUTNEY

This simple chutney will enliven any dal. The pineapple and mint are also good for digestion. Chili pepper is more traditional in this recipe than jalapeño, but I had jalapeños in my garden and they did the job just fine. In fact, I had a red one, which looked very pretty in the yellow and green chutney. (Unless you garden, you may not know that jalapeños turn red when they are ripe.)

Yield: About 1^1/$_3$ Cup

^{1}/$_2$ cup pineapple juice

1 cup pineapple pulp

^{1}/$_4$ cup coarsely chopped onion

^{1}/$_3$ cup mint leaves

1 chili or jalapeño pepper, minced

1. In a blender, combine the pineapple juice, pineapple pulp, onion, mint leaves, and chili pepper. Blend until fairly smooth.

2. Serve the chutney immediately with a curry dish, or store it in a covered container in the refrigerator for up to 1 week. Allow the chutney to return to room temperature before serving from the refrigerator.

Pretty Smart

Juice according to the seasons and you will save money on produce while giving your body a healthy variety of nutrients. In winter, emphasize apples, carrots, beets, and cabbage juice. Warm these juices up with a little ginger or even a pinch of cayenne pepper. In summer, focus on cucumbers, celery, tomatoes, and melons. Add fennel and mint to summer juices to make them even more refreshing and cooling.

SPINACH PULP PESTO

Unlike typical homemade pesto that turns brown so quickly, this version holds its color beautifully. I once served it over mashed winter squash and a bed of red quinoa with a few toasted pumpkin seeds as garnish. It was as pretty as it was delicious.

Yield: 1 Cup

1 cup lightly packed fresh basil	1 clove garlic
$1/4$ cup spinach juice	$1/4$ cup olive oil
$1/2$ cup spinach pulp	$1/2$ teaspoon sea salt
$1/2$ cup pumpkin seeds	$1/4$ cup nutritional yeast

1. In a blender, combine the basil, spinach juice, spinach pulp, pumpkin seeds, garlic, olive oil, and sea salt. Blend until desired consistency is achieved, using a spatula to scrape the sides of the blender as needed.

2. In a medium-sized mixing bowl, combine the pesto and nutritional yeast. Mix well and serve.

Helpful Tip

For a beautiful canapé, spread $1^1/2$-inch squares of whole grain focaccia with this pesto, topping each one with a sliver of sundried tomato.

The Difference is Huge

Store anything that contains whole grains, nuts, seeds, or oils in the refrigerator or freezer to prevent it from going rancid before you use it. This includes flours, nuts, cereals, chips, crackers, and brown rice.

CASHEW SANDWICH SPREAD

This simple spread is great on toast or crackers. While I use a mixture of carrot, cucumber, and celery pulp, just about any vegetable pulp will do.

Yield: About 2 Cups

1 cup cashews

$1/_3$ cup carrot pulp

$1/_3$ cup cucumber pulp

$1/_3$ cup celery pulp

$1/_4$ cup coarsely chopped sweet onion or scallions

2 tablespoons lime juice

$1/_2$ teaspoon fennel seed

$1/_4$ teaspoon salt, or to taste

1. In a medium-sized mixing bowl, cover the cashews with water by 1 inch. Allow them to soak for at least 2 hours or up to 8 hours. Drain and rinse the cashews.

2. In a food processor or high-powered blender, combine the cashews, carrot pulp, cucumber pulp, celery pulp, sweet onion, lime juice, fennel seed, and salt. Process until the cashews are coarsely ground.

3. Store the spread in a covered container in the refrigerator for up to 3 days.

Helpful Tip

If you do not have a food processor or high-powered blender, an ordinary blender will work, but you will need to blend the mixture in 3 or 4 batches, using a spatula to scrape the sides of the blender as needed.

BAKED OLIVE PÂTÉ

This pâté may be sliced and served on a bed of greens or spread on crackers as a tasty appetizer. I used carrot and spinach pulp for this recipe, but all-carrot pulp or another veggie mixture would work.

Yield: 9 Squares

6-ounce can pitted black olives, drained

$1/4$ cup carrot juice or vegetable broth

$1/4$ cup spinach juice, water, or vegetable broth

$1/2$ cup spinach pulp

$1/3$ cup coarsely chopped onion

2 tablespoons chickpea flour

2 to 3 cloves garlic, peeled

2 tablespoons tamari

2 tablespoons freshly chopped rosemary, or 1 teaspoon dried

1 teaspoon smoked paprika

$1/4$ white pepper

$1/2$ cup carrot pulp

1. Preheat the oven to 350°F. Grease an 8-x-8-inch baking pan with olive oil and sprinkle it with flour. Set aside.

2. In a blender, combine the olives, carrot juice, spinach juice, spinach pulp, onion, chickpea flour, garlic, tamari, rosemary, smoked paprika, and white pepper. Blend until smooth.

3. In a large mixing bowl, combine the blended mixture and carrot pulp. Mix well.

4. Spread the mixture evenly in the prepared baking pan. Bake for 30 minutes, or until firm. Cut the pâté into squares. Serve at room temperature or chilled.

SHIITAKE PÂTÉ

Dried mushrooms have more flavor than fresh, as this scrumptious pâté proves. Serve it on a bed of vinaigrette-dressed salad greens as an elegant starter, or make a great sandwich by thickly spreading it on whole grain bread, adding a little Dijon mustard, and topping everything with baby arugula.

Yield: 9 Squares

2 cups dehydrated whole shiitake mushrooms (about 2 ounces)

2 cups lukewarm water

$1/4$ cup vegetable juice

1 cup vegetable pulp

1 cup almonds

$1/3$ cup onion

$1/2$ cup rolled oats

1 tablespoon freshly grated ginger

3 tablespoons tamari

1 teaspoon thyme

$1/2$ teaspoon white pepper

1. In a medium-sized mixing bowl, cover the mushrooms with the water. Allow them to soak for 30 minutes, or until rehydrated.

2. Preheat the oven to 350°F. Grease an 8-x-8-inch baking pan with olive oil and sprinkle it with flour. Set aside.

3. Drain the mushrooms through a coffee filter or cheesecloth, reserving the water. (If needed, add more water to yield 1 cup water.) Rinse the mushrooms. Cut off and discard the mushroom stems.

4. In a food processor, combine the mushrooms, reserved water, vegetable juice, vegetable pulp, almonds, onion, rolled oats, ginger, tamari, thyme, and white pepper. Blend until smooth.

5. Spread the mixture evenly in the prepared baking pan. Bake for 30 minutes, or until firm. Cut the pâté into squares. Serve at room temperature or chilled.

TAHINI VEGETABLE SPREAD

This is an old favorite revised to use pulp instead of grated carrots. It is delicious spread on toast and eaten with soup or salad.

Yield: About 1 Cup

$1/2$ cup tahini

2 tablespoons water or carrot juice

1 tablespoon balsamic vinegar

1 tablespoon tamari, or to taste

1 cup carrot pulp

$1/4$ cup nutritional yeast

1 to 2 cloves garlic, pressed

1. In a medium-sized mixing bowl, combine the tahini, water, balsamic vinegar, and tamari. Mix well until thick and creamy.

2. Add the carrot pulp, nutritional yeast, and garlic to the bowl. Mix well. If the spread is too dry, add 1 additional tablespoon water or juice.

For a Change . . .

Instead of all-carrot pulp, try a combination of carrot pulp, cabbage pulp, and fennel pulp.

The Little Differences

"Not too sweet but sweet enough" is my rule of thumb when juicing. Experts in nutritional healing agree that too much sugar, even natural sugar, is not good for you. Carrots today have been hybridized to be extremely sweet, but you can cut this sweetness by using other vegetables such as cucumber, cabbage, celery, or tomato in combination with carrots.

WHITE BEAN AND SPINACH DIP

This dip is delicious with pita chips or bread, but it is also lovely on a bed of salad greens accompanied by some steamed asparagus as a light meal.

Yield: 2 Cups

2 cups cooked cannellini beans or other white beans

$1/4$ cup spinach juice

$1/2$ cup spinach pulp

2 tablespoons olive oil

2 tablespoons balsamic vinegar

$1/2$ teaspoon salt, or to taste

1. In a blender, combine the cannellini beans, spinach juice, spinach pulp, olive oil, balsamic vinegar, and salt. Blend until desired consistency is achieved, using a spatula to scrape the sides of the blender as needed. If necessary, add slightly more juice.

2. Serve immediately, or chill in the refrigerator before serving.

For a Change . . .

Instead of spinach pulp, try using $1/4$ cup carrot pulp. Add $1/4$ cup carrot juice for extra flavor.

Pretty Smart

This is a no-fail way to make most vegetable, bean, or grain dishes taste good in a hurry: Add tamari or soy sauce, balsamic vinegar, and white pepper in judicious amounts.

PAPAYA SAUCE

We grow papaya in our garden, and it's one of our favorite fruits because it is so rich in vitamins and enzymes. Use this unsweetened fruit sauce over pancakes, cakes, or other desserts.

Yield: 1$^1/_2$ Cups

$^1/_2$ lemon, halved   Stevia to taste (optional)

**1 ripe medium-sized papaya,
   peeled and seeded**

1. Juice the lemon and papaya. Reserve the juice and pulp.

2. In a medium-sized mixing bowl, combine the lemon and papaya juice and pulp. Mix well.

3. If you would like a sweeter sauce, add Stevia to the bowl and mix well. Store the sauce in a covered container in the refrigerator for up to 3 days.

PEAR SAUCE

Use this sauce over plain cake, fruit salad, pancakes, or waffles. It is fresh, light, and flavorful.

Yield: 1$^1/_2$ Cups

$^1/_2$-inch piece ginger   **3 pears, cored and sliced**

$^1/_2$ lemon, halved   Stevia to taste (optional)

1. Juice the ginger, lemon, and pears. Reserve the juice and pulp.

2. In a medium-sized mixing bowl, combine the ginger, lemon, and pear juice and pulp. Mix well.

3. If you would like a sweeter sauce, add Stevia to the bowl and mix well. Store the sauce in a covered container in the refrigerator for up to 3 days.

6

The Path of
the Righteous
Main Dishes

Pulp can be hidden in every meal, from sweet breakfast dishes to savory lunches and dinners. Generally, I use fruit pulp for breakfast and vegetable pulp for the other two meals of the day. Vegetable pulp, with its mild flavor, may be used in a variety of main dishes, serving as nutritious filler in vegan main-dish recipes—especially in veggie burgers. Veggie burgers are easy to make, most everyone likes them, and pulp gives them a firm texture. I included several burger and patty-type recipes in this chapter in order to offer a wide variety of options and flavors in regard to this type of dish. There are so many different food preferences out there that it is helpful to explore different ways of doing similar recipes. Another advantage of having several recipes for the same kind of dish is that it becomes a lot easier to improvise and come up with your own versions of these burgers once you've made a bunch of them. We learn by doing, and this is what this book is all about: empowering the reader to learn how to cook, not just follow recipes.

But no one should live on burgers alone, of course, so there are several other dishes in this chapter that turn pulp into dinner or lunch. There are pulp balls, which you may serve with or without pasta and tomato sauce; delicious pulp quiche, which you don't have to be vegan to enjoy; and even a few great curry dishes, which are among my favorites. No matter the meal, every recipe in this section will help you turn your high-fiber juicing pulp into dishes you and your loved ones are sure to enjoy.

CABBAGE AND COCONUT CURRY

The humble cabbage is a perfect vegetable to juice because it is relatively mild and so good for you. If you can find kaffir lime leaves, I highly recommend adding them as a wonderful additional flavor.

Yield: 4 to 6 Servings

1 tablespoon coconut oil

1$^1/_2$ cups coarsely chopped onion

4 cups finely chopped cabbage

4 cups sliced carrots ($^3/_4$-inch slices)

1 cup cabbage pulp

1 to 2 tablespoons grated ginger

1 teaspoon ground cumin

$^1/_2$ teaspoon ground cardamom

$^1/_2$ teaspoon turmeric

$^1/_2$ teaspoon ground fenugreek

4 kaffir lime leaves (optional)

1 teaspoon salt

1 cup water or cabbage juice

1 to 2 tablespoons apple cider vinegar, or to taste

$^1/_2$ cup coconut cream

Pinch of cayenne pepper

1. In a 6-quart Dutch oven, heat the coconut oil over medium heat. Add the onion. Cover and cook while you chop the cabbage and carrots, or for about 5 minutes.

2. Add the chopped cabbage, sliced carrots, cabbage pulp, ginger, cumin, cardamom, turmeric, fenugreek, kaffir lime leaves, and salt to the Dutch oven. Stir gently. Cover and cook for 5 minutes, or until the mixture needs water to keep it from getting scorched.

3. Add the water and vinegar to the Dutch oven. Stir gently. Cover and cook for about 30 minutes, or until the vegetables are tender. If needed, add a little more water to keep it from scorching. Stir in the coconut cream and cayenne pepper. Mix well and serve.

Helpful Tip

If you don't want to deal with the long list of spices, just use 1 heaping tablespoon curry powder instead.

CAULIFLOWER CURRY

This curry can be a lovely a base for an Indian meal when served over brown basmati rice and accompanied by a bean dish.

Yield: 4 Servings

1 recipe Tomato Curry Sauce
(page 80)

1 large cauliflower, cut into florets

Salt to taste

Cayenne pepper to taste

1. In a heavy $4^1/_2$-quart Dutch oven, prepare the tomato curry sauce. Cook it down for only 5 minutes, not by half, as the recipe instructs.

2. Add the cauliflower to the saucepan. Cover and cook over low heat, stirring occasionally, for about 20 minutes, or until the cauliflower is tender. Stir in the salt and cayenne pepper. Serve.

DAL

Dal is a curried bean dish. It is a staple of the Indian diet and a major source of protein in India. This recipe is not only delicious but also full of healthful phytonutrients.

Yield: 4 Servings

1 recipe Tomato Curry Sauce
(page 80)

2 cups cooked green lentils,
red lentils, or mung beans

Salt to taste

Cayenne pepper to taste

1. In a $4^1/_2$-quart Dutch oven, prepare the tomato curry sauce.

2. Add the cooked lentils to the saucepan. Simmer for about 5 minutes. Stir in the salt and cayenne pepper. Serve.

QUINOA CURRY

This curry is delicious as a base for steamed vegetables or dal. Although quinoa is not a traditional ingredient in Indian cuisine, it works nicely with curry spices and other Indian foods.

Yield: 4 Servings

1 tablespoon olive oil

$1/4$ cup finely chopped onion

1 tablespoon curry powder

1 cup quinoa

1 cup vegetable pulp

$1/2$ teaspoon salt

2 cups water, or $1^1/2$ cups water and $1/2$ cup vegetable juice

1. In a 12-inch skillet, heat the olive oil over medium heat. Add the onion and sauté for 5 minutes, or until the onion is translucent.

2. Add the curry powder, quinoa, vegetable pulp, and salt to the skillet. Stir over medium-high heat for 1 minute, or until very hot.

3. Add the water to the skillet, stir, cover, and reduce the heat to low. Simmer for about 20 minutes, or until the liquid has been absorbed. Serve.

Pretty Smart

Truffle oil may be used to get the marvelous flavor of truffle into a dish without actually having the real thing on hand. I sometimes combine truffle oil, vinegar, and tamari in a recipe, and even add a little nutritional yeast, which enhances these flavors. This combination is great in sauces and gravies for pulp burgers.

BLACK BEAN AND BEET BURGERS

Not long ago, friends from my local organic farm were talking about an amazing black bean and beet burger recipe that was circulating, but I never actually got it. To correct this problem, I created my own version using pulp. This burger goes especially well with salsa and salad.

Yield: 8 Burgers

$1^1/_2$ cup cooked black beans

1 cup rolled oats

1 cup beet pulp or mixed beet and carrot pulp

$1/_4$ cup minced sweet onion

$1/_3$ cup finely chopped bell pepper

$1/_2$ minced jalapeño pepper, or to taste

1 teaspoon salt

1 teaspoon basil

1 teaspoon smoked paprika

$1/_2$ teaspoon cumin

2 tablespoons olive oil, divided

1. In a food processor, combine the black beans and rolled oats. Purée just enough to create a mixture that holds together.

2. In a large mixing bowl, combine the bean and oat mixture, beet pulp, sweet onion, bell pepper, jalapeño pepper, salt, basil, smoked paprika, and cumin. Mix well, using your hands. Shape into 8 patties of equal size, pressing firmly.

3. In a 12-inch skillet, heat 1 tablespoon olive oil over medium heat. Cook 4 patties for about 5 minutes, or until each patty is browned on the bottom. Flip them and cook until crispy brown. Set aside the cooked patties.

4. Repeat step 3 with the remaining patties.

CHICKPEA CROQUETTES

This falafel-inspired croquette is enriched with both juice and pulp, and is sure to impress. As you will see, there is no need to deep fry the croquettes; pan frying will do just fine. They go well with Almost Instant Tomato Sauce (page 81) and salad.

Yield: 9 Croquettes

1$^1/_2$ cup cooked chickpeas	1 teaspoon salt
$^1/_4$ cup carrot juice	2 cloves garlic, pressed
1$^1/_2$ cup vegetable pulp	$^1/_4$ cup tahini
1 cup whole grain bread crumbs	2 tablespoons olive oil, divided
1 teaspoon cumin	

1. In a large mixing bowl, mash the chickpeas with a potato masher.

2. Add the carrot juice, vegetable pulp, bread crumbs, cumin, salt, garlic, and tahini to the large mixing bowl. Mix well, using your hands if necessary. Shape into 9 croquettes of equal size, pressing firmly.

3. In a 12-inch skillet, heat 1 tablespoon olive oil over medium heat. Cook 4 croquettes for about 5 minutes, or until each patty is browned on the bottom. Flip them and cook until crispy brown. Set aside the cooked croquettes.

4. Repeat step 3 with the remaining croquettes.

That's All You Had to Say

I once contacted the Center for Science in the Public Interest to ask if there was anything unhealthy about liquid smoke. They did a bit of research for me and couldn't come up with any concerns. I sometimes use liquid smoke in bean, tofu, or tempeh dishes, and have been known to add it to pulp burgers and stews.

FAUX SALMON PATTIES

Adding dulse flakes to a mixture of carrot and beet pulp not only adds a healthy dose of minerals to this recipe, but also reminds me of the little salmon patties my mother used to make. This patty goes perfectly with a green salad and some whole grain bread, or even a grain dish.

Yield: 8 Patties

$3/4$ cup red lentils, picked over and rinsed

$1^1/_2$ cup water

$1/_2$ cup carrot pulp

$1/_2$ cup beet pulp

$1/_2$ cup dulse flakes

$1/_4$ cup minced onion

$1/_2$ teaspoon salt, or to taste

Freshly ground black pepper to taste

$1/_4$ cup millet flour or other whole grain flour

2 tablespoons olive oil, divided

1. In a $2^1/_2$-quart saucepan, cover the lentils with the water. Bring to a boil. Reduce the heat to low, cover, and simmer for about 15 minutes, or until the water has been absorbed and the lentils form a purée.

2. In a large mixing bowl, combine the cooked lentils, carrot pulp, beet pulp, dulse flakes, minced onion, salt, and black pepper. Mix well, using your hands if necessary. Shape into 8 patties of equal size.

3. Place the flour on a small plate. Dredge each patty in the flour and set aside.

4. In a 12-inch skillet, heat 1 tablespoon olive oil over medium heat. Cook 4 patties for about 5 minutes, or until each patty is browned on the bottom. Flip them and cook until crispy brown. Set aside the cooked patties.

5. Repeat step 4 with the remaining patties.

HIPPY PULP BURGERS

Hemp seeds, tofu, brown rice, and nutritional yeast may seem a bit "crunchy" to the culinary sophisticates out there, but this burger is delicious and nutritious nonetheless. Just give it a try it and I'm sure you'll agree.

Yield: 8 Burgers

1 pound firm tofu	1 to 3 cloves garlic, pressed
1 cup vegetable pulp	1 teaspoon salt
1 cup cooked brown rice	1 teaspoon thyme
$1/2$ cup hemp seeds	$1/2$ teaspoon white pepper
$1/3$ cup nutritional yeast	2 tablespoons olive oil, divided
$1/3$ cup finely chopped onion or scallions	

1. Hold the tofu over the sink and squeeze it with your hands to press out the excess water. In a large mixing bowl, mash the tofu with a potato masher.

2. Add the vegetable pulp, brown rice, hemp seeds, nutritional yeast, onion, garlic, salt, thyme, and white pepper to the large mixing bowl. Mix well, using your hands if necessary.

3. Shape the mixture into 8 patties of equal size, pressing firmly.

4. In a 12-inch skillet, heat 1 tablespoon olive oil over medium heat. Cook 4 patties for about 5 minutes, or until each patty is browned on the bottom. Flip them and cook until crispy brown. Set aside the cooked burgers.

5. Repeat step 4 with the remaining patties.

SPICY KIDNEY BEAN BURGERS

This burger has a nice, firm texture and a lovely touch of spice. It is good on a bun, topped with lettuce, tomato, and avocado slices, or alongside rice, salsa, and salad. If you'd like a little more heat, serve it with a few pickled jalapeño peppers.

Yield: 4 Burgers

$1/2$ cup toasted unsalted pumpkin seeds

$1/2$ cup sundried tomatoes

$1^1/2$ cups cooked kidney beans

1 cup vegetable pulp

1 tablespoon tamari

$1/3$ cup minced sweet onion

1 teaspoon basil

1 teaspoon cumin

$1/2$ teaspoon ground chipotle

$1/4$ cup cornmeal

1 tablespoon olive oil

1. Place the pumpkin seeds in a blender and coarsely grind. Add the sundried tomatoes and coarsely grind.

2. In a large mixing bowl, combine the pumpkin seed and tomato mixture and the kidney beans. Mash with a potato masher until the mixture holds together.

3. Add the vegetable pulp, tamari, sweet onion, basil, cumin, and chipotle to the large mixing bowl. Mix well, using your hands if necessary. Shape into 4 patties of equal size, pressing firmly.

4. Place the cornmeal on a small plate. Dredge each patty in the cornmeal and set aside.

5. In a 12-inch skillet, heat the olive oil over medium heat. Cook the patties for about 5 minutes, or until each patty is browned on the bottom. Flip them and cook for another 5 minutes, or until crispy brown.

TEMPEH BURGERS

This burger is quite easy to make, and even my most finicky friend enjoys it, so it must be pretty good.

Yield: 8 Burgers

8 ounces tempeh

1 cup vegetable pulp

$1/4$ cup minced onion or scallions

$1/4$ cup nutritional yeast

2 tablespoons crunchy peanut butter

1 clove garlic, pressed

1 teaspoon herbes de Provence

$1/2$ teaspoon salt, or to taste

2 tablespoons olive oil, divided

1. Slice the tempeh into 4 equal pieces and steam them for about 10 minutes.

2. In a large mixing bowl, combine the tempeh, vegetable pulp, onion, nutritional yeast, peanut butter, garlic, herbes de Provence, and salt. Mix well, using your hands if necessary. Shape into 8 patties of equal size.

3. In a 12-inch skillet, heat 1 tablespoon olive oil over medium heat. Cook 4 patties for about 5 minutes, or until each patty is browned on the bottom. Flip them and cook for another 5 minutes, or until crispy brown. Set aside the cooked burgers.

4. Repeat step 3 with the remaining patties.

TOFU-PULP BURGERS

I made these burgers for dinner guests and they were eaten with glee. It is a fairly large recipe, so you can cut it in half if you like.

Yield: 12 Burgers

15 ounces extra-firm tofu

2 cups vegetable pulp

2 cups whole grain bread crumbs

$1/_2$ cup coarsely ground almonds

$1/_2$ cup nutritional yeast

$1/_4$ cup tamari

1 teaspoon thyme

3 tablespoons olive oil, divided

1 recipe Quick Mushroom Sauce (page 83)

1. Hold the tofu over the sink and squeeze it with your hands to press out the excess water. In a large mixing bowl, mash the tofu with a potato masher.

2. Add the vegetable pulp, bread crumbs, almonds, yeast, tamari, and thyme to the large mixing bowl. Mix well, using your hands if necessary. Shape into 12 patties of equal size, pressing firmly.

3. In a 12-inch skillet, heat 1 tablespoon olive oil over medium heat. Cook 4 patties for about 5 minutes, or until each patty is browned on the bottom. Flip them and cook for another 5 minutes, or until crispy brown. Set aside the cooked patties.

4. Repeat step 3 until you have cooked all 12 patties. Serve with the mushroom sauce.

PULP PIE

A quiche turned vegan and made with Japanese and Italian ingredients—call it "pulp fusion." This dish holds together nicely and presents beautifully. Serve it with salad for a simple yet elegant meal.

Yield: One 9-Inch Pie

1 Gluten-Free Savory Pie Crust (page 54) or other prepared crust

15-ounces extra-firm tofu, pressed

1 cup carrot pulp

$1/2$ cup sliced pitted black olives

$1/4$ cup chopped sundried tomatoes

2 tablespoons dried onion flakes

1 teaspoon basil

1 teaspoon oregano

1 teaspoon turmeric

3 to 4 cloves garlic, pressed

$1/2$ teaspoon salt, or to taste

12-ounce bunch fresh asparagus, trimmed

1 teaspoon olive oil

1. Preheat the oven to 375°F.

2. Hold the tofu over the sink and squeeze it with your hands to press out the excess water. Place the tofu in a food processor. Process until smooth.

3. Transfer the tofu to a large mixing bowl. Add the carrot pulp. Mix well, using your hands if necessary, until the mixture holds together.

4. Add the olives, sundried tomatoes, onion flakes, basil, oregano, turmeric, garlic, and salt to the large mixing bowl. Mix well.

5. Cut the tops of the asparagus spears by about 3 inches. Set aside. Slice the remaining bottom parts into $1/2$-inch pieces. Add the bottom pieces to the large mixing bowl. Mix well.

6. Spoon the mixture into the pie crust, pressing it down firmly and evenly. Arrange the asparagus spears over top, pressing them down firmly. Drizzle the olive oil over the asparagus spears.

7. Place the pie on the bottom rack of the oven and bake for 40 minutes, or until the pie is firm and the crust is brown. Allow the pie to cool for about 10 minutes before slicing and serving.

Helpful Tip

If you are mashing the tofu with a potato masher, you will probably need to get your hands into the mixture and squish it to get it to stick together.

GOLDEN PULP BALLS

These balls are full of flavor and hold together well. Try them with Almost Instant Tomato Sauce (page 81) and pasta for an amazing dinner.

Yield: About 20 Balls

8 ounces extra-firm tofu

$1^3/_4$ cup whole grain bread crumbs

1 cup vegetable pulp

$^1/_4$ cup minced onion

$^1/_4$ cup crunchy peanut butter

2 to 3 cloves garlic, pressed

1 teaspoon sage

1 teaspoon salt

$^1/_2$ teaspoon white pepper

$^1/_2$ teaspoon turmeric

1. Preheat the oven to 350°F. Generously grease an 18-x-13-inch baking sheet with olive oil. Set aside.

2. Hold the tofu over the sink and squeeze it with your hands to press out the excess water. In a large mixing bowl, mash the tofu with a potato masher.

3. Add the bread crumbs, vegetable pulp, onion, peanut butter, garlic, sage, salt, white pepper, and turmeric to the large mixing bowl. Mix well, using your hands if necessary. Shape into 20 balls of equal size, pressing firmly.

4. Place the balls on the prepared baking sheet. Brush or lightly spray the tops of the balls with olive oil. Bake for about 45 minutes.

Helpful Tip

Reheat balls in a covered skillet with a small amount of olive oil over medium heat or in a toaster oven. When serving these balls with sauce, set them on top of the sauce. Don't mix them into the sauce, as they will get soggy.

GREEN MASHED POTATOES

Serve these on St. Patrick's Day, or any other day, really! Add another color to this recipe by coupling it with Fuchsia Velouté Sauce (page 82), and make a meal of it by serving it with a tempeh or tofu dish and salad.

Yield: 6 Servings

$2^1/_2$ pounds potatoes, diced	2 tablespoons olive oil
5 ounces baby spinach	$^1/_2$ teaspoon salt
$^1/_4$ cup chopped fresh dill weed (optional)	Freshly ground black pepper to taste

1. In a 6-quart Dutch oven, combine the potatoes and 2 inches water. Cover and bring to a boil. Reduce the heat to medium-low and cook for 20 minutes, or until the potatoes are tender. If necessary, add $^1/_2$ cup more water to keep them from scorching. When the potatoes are done, the amount of water remaining should be just enough to mash them. If it looks like there is too much, drain some of it. Mash the potatoes right in the pan.

2. Juice the spinach. Add the spinach juice and spinach pulp to the Dutch oven. Mix well. If necessary, add more juice, water, or some unsweetened soy milk to achieve the desired consistency.

3. Add the dill weed, olive oil, salt, and black pepper. Mix well.

For a Change . . .

If you don't care for dill weed, or if it is not in season, use parsley, chives, or minced scallions instead.

Helpful Tip

This is the way I cook mashed potatoes. The outcome can vary depending on pan, potatoes, and temperature, so it is not an exact science. The cooking liquid adds flavor and minerals, and no one seems to miss the butter and milk. If you are prone to burning what you cook, you may want to boil the potatoes in the conventional manner and drain the liquid.

SUMMER SQUASH CASSEROLE

This dish is reminiscent of an old Southern dish I remember eating as a kid. I added some corn to give it texture and sweetness. It is a good example of what I mean when I talk about using your juicer as a kitchen tool, as the cashews, which create the creaminess, are blended with the squash juice and then mixed with the pulp.

Yield: 6 Servings

2 slices whole grain bread, torn into small pieces

$1/2$ cup coarsely chopped shallots or onion

2 pounds yellow summer squash (about 5 medium-sized)

$1/2$ cup cashews

$1/2$ cup garbanzo flour

1 teaspoon salt

$1^1/2$ cup sweet corn

$1/2$ cup nutritional yeast

1 teaspoon basil

Freshly ground black pepper to taste

1. Preheat oven to 350°F. Grease an 8-x-12-inch casserole dish with olive oil. Set aside.

2. In a food processor or blender, combine the bread and shallots. Process coarsely. Set aside.

3. Juice the squash. Reserve the juice and pulp separately.

4. In a blender, combine the reserved squash juice and cashews. Blend until smooth. Add the garbanzo flour and salt. Blend again until smooth. Transfer all but $1/3$ cup mixture to a large mixing bowl.

5. Add the reserved squash pulp and corn to the large mixing bowl. Mix well. Transfer the mixture to the prepared casserole dish.

6. Sprinkle the prepared bread crumbs over the casserole and drizzle it with the reserved blended mixture. Sprinkle the nutritional yeast, basil, and black pepper over the casserole and bake for 45 minutes, or until brown and crispy on top and somewhat firm. Allow the casserole to sit for 10 minutes before serving.

LENTIL-WALNUT PULP LOAF

This hearty loaf is great when served with steamed vegetables, Almost Instant Tomato Sauce (page 81), and salad.

Yield: 6 Servings

1 cup red lentils, picked over and rinsed	1 cup chopped walnuts, divided
2 cups water	$1/3$ cup dried onion flakes
$1/2$ cup and 3 tablespoons rolled oats, divided	1 teaspoon salt
	1 teaspoon sage
1 cup carrot pulp	$1/2$ cup tomato purée

1. In a $4^1/2$-quart saucepan, combine the lentils and water. Bring to a boil, reduce the heat to low, and simmer for 15 to 20 minutes, or until the water is absorbed and the lentils form a purée.

2. Preheat the oven to 350°F. Grease a 9-x-5-inch loaf pan with olive oil and sprinkle it with 3 tablespoons rolled oats to coat the bottom and sides. Set aside.

3. In a large mixing bowl, combine the cooked lentils and carrot pulp. Add $3/4$ cup walnuts, reserving $1/4$ cup for the top of the loaf. Add the remaining $1/2$ cup rolled oats, onion flakes, salt, and sage. Mix well.

4. Transfer the mixture to the prepared loaf pan, pressing it down firmly. Place the reserved $1/4$ cup walnuts on top of the loaf, distributing them evenly and pressing them down slightly. Spread the tomato purée on top of the loaf.

5. Bake for 50 to 60 minutes. Allow the loaf to sit for 5 minutes. Loosen the sides of the loaf with a knife and transfer it to a serving platter.

7

Any Time of the Day Is a Good Time for Pie . . . and Other Desserts

Fruit makes the perfect healthy dessert or sweet treat. In a pulp kitchen, we can take advantage of the sweetness left in fruit pulp—as well as in carrot pulp or beet pulp—to enhance a variety of dessert recipes. And you could always add a little juice back to the pulp to give a recipe more flavor and a nutritional boost. Just as pulp adds moistness and fiber to breads and muffins, so it adds these same qualities to cakes and brownies. Moreover, I am excited for you to discover that desserts without refined flours, refined sweeteners, or animal products can taste just as good as—or better than—their conventionally prepared versions.

These recipes have been kept as low in added fats and sweeteners as possible while still making them desserts. Desserts and sweets are special, and no one wants to eat a dessert that tastes like cardboard, no matter how healthy it is. I find that most desserts, however, even those from health food stores, are typically too sweet. The levels of sweetness found in the following recipes are closer to what you might find in a dessert in France or Italy, although the dishes here are more nutritious because they use fewer refined ingredients. There is no reason desserts cannot be high in nourishment and still be a treat.

The sorbets in this chapter are definitely worth a try. You can follow one of the included recipes, or use the instructions as a guideline to create your own sorbet with whichever type of fruit juice and pulp you have on hand. Enjoy!

PAPAYA PIE

The amazing thing about this pie, aside from its fabulous flavor, is that it is totally raw but has a creamy texture that holds up for slicing.

Yield: One 9-Inch Pie

1 recipe Almond Pie Crust (page 53)

1 medium-sized papaya, peeled and seeded (about 2 to 2^1/$_2$ pounds)

^{1}/$_2$ cup soft pitted dates

^{1}/$_4$ cup coconut butter

1. Prepare the pie crust. Set aside.

2. Slice the papaya into strips and juice them. Reserve 2 cups papaya juice and all the papaya pulp.

3. In a blender, combine the reserved papaya juice, dates, and coconut butter. Blend until very smooth and creamy.

4. In a medium-sized mixing bowl, combine the papaya mixture and the reserved papaya pulp. Mix well and pour into the pie crust. Refrigerate for at least 3 hours before serving.

Correctamundo

I have discovered that almost any type of fruit pulp will make a delicious pie—not a thick gooey pie, but a thin, delicious pie with a crispy crust. Because pulp is drier than whole fruit, it actually allows the crust to become crisp, which really makes it good. Start with a high-quality crust, spread fruit pulp along the bottom, add sweetener such as maple syrup over the pulp, and drizzle just a little coconut oil on top if desired. Sprinkle on some chopped nuts, if you'd like, and bake it on the bottom rack of the oven at 350°F for about 30 minutes, or until the crust is brown and crispy.

PECAN AND PEAR PULP PIE

This is not a thick, gooey pie, but rather more like a French tart. If you plan to serve it warm with vanilla ice cream, it will be gently sweet and truly delightful. If you plan to serve it alone, you should probably use 4 rather than 2 tablespoons maple syrup.

Yield: One 9-Inch Pie

1 recipe Gluten-Free Sweet Pie Crust (page 55)

1 cup pear pulp

2 tablespoons arrowroot powder

1 cup pecans

2 to 4 tablespoons maple syrup

1. Preheat the oven to 375°F.

2. Prepare the pie crust. Place the pie crust in the refrigerator until needed.

3. In a large mixing bowl, combine the pear pulp and arrowroot powder. Mix well to dissolve the arrowroot powder. Spread the mixture over the bottom of the pie crust.

4. Distribute the pecans evenly over the pulp mixture, pressing them in gently. Drizzle the maple syrup over the pie. Bake on the bottom rack of the oven for about 40 minutes, or until the crust is crispy brown and the filling is firm. Allow the pie to cool for 10 to 15 minutes before serving.

Helpful Tip

This recipe requires very good pears, so wait until they are in season to make it.

Correctamundo

Sunflower sprouts are great in green juice, carrot juice, beet juice, or even fruit juice. They are mildly flavored and provide a nice dose of chlorophyll and other nutrients.

COCONUT COOKIES

These cookies are very high in protein and fiber, and have no gluten whatsoever. They make a nice treat to serve with coffee or tea.

Yield: 20 Cookies

1 cup chickpea flour

2 teaspoons baking powder

$1/4$ teaspoon baking soda

1 cup carrot pulp

1 cup unsweetened shredded coconut

$1/3$ cup coconut butter

$1/3$ cup maple syrup or coconut nectar

2 teaspoons vanilla extract

1 to 2 drops Stevia, or to taste

1. Preheat the oven to 350°F. Grease a 12-x-17-inch baking sheet with coconut oil and sprinkle it with flour. Set aside.

2. In a large mixing bowl, combine the chickpea flour, baking powder, and baking soda. Mix well.

3. Add the carrot pulp and shredded coconut to the large mixing bowl. Mix well to distribute them evenly, using your hands if necessary. Set aside.

4. In a medium-sized mixing bowl, combine the coconut butter, maple syrup, vanilla extract, and Stevia. Mix well.

5. Add the wet ingredients to the dry ingredients. Knead until dough forms.

6. On a work surface, roll the dough into a 10-inch log. Cut the log into 20 cookies using a knife dipped in cool water. Place the cookies on the prepared baking sheet, flattening them slightly with a fork dipped in water. Bake for 10 to 15 minutes, or until firm and lightly browned on the bottom.

Helpful Tip

These cookies may be eaten warm out of the oven, but if you'd like them to be a little crispy, leave them in the oven after you've turned it off until they've dried out a bit.

ALMOND COOKIES

These almond cookies are delicious, easy to make, and do not contain any gluten. Serve them with some hot tea for a perfect afternoon snack.

Yield: 18 Cookies

$1/2$ cup almond butter	$1/2$ teaspoon almond extract
3 tablespoons coconut oil	$1/2$ cup garbanzo flour
$1/3$ cup maple syrup	1 teaspoon baking powder
$1/2$ cup carrot pulp or apple pulp	

1. Preheat the oven to 350°F. Grease a 12-x-17-inch baking sheet with coconut oil. Set aside.

2. In a large mixing bowl, combine the almond butter and coconut oil. Stir in the maple syrup. Add the carrot pulp and almond extract. Mix well.

3. In a small mixing bowl, combine the garbanzo flour and baking powder. Add the dry ingredients to the large mixing bowl. Mix well until dough forms.

4. Drop the batter by the heaping teaspoon onto the prepared baking sheet, leaving at least 1 inch between drops. Bake for 10 to 12 minutes, or until firm and lightly browned.

RAW CARROT-GINGER COOKIES

Inspired by my friend Steven Shepard, these raw cookies couldn't be easier to make. They are thin and crisp, with a hint of maple and ginger.

Yield: 24 Cookies

1 cup walnut halves $1/2$-inch piece ginger, juiced

$1/3$ cup carrot juice $1/3$ cup maple syrup

$1^1/_2$ cups carrot pulp

1. In a blender or food processor, grind the walnuts finely but not into a powder.

2. In a large mixing bowl, combine the ground walnuts, carrot juice, carrot pulp, ginger juice, and maple syrup. Mix well.

3. Drop the batter by the heaping teaspoon onto nonstick mesh dehydrator sheets. Using the back of a fork, flatten out each mound to about $1/4$-inch in thickness. Dip the fork in water to keep it from sticking.

4. Dehydrate the sheets at 110°F for about 12 hours, or until very crisp. Allow the cookies to cool to room temperature before serving.

Correctamundo

Don't fall for food fads or commercial hype. When you scrutinize a food trend, first look at the science as reported by legitimate institutions such as universities, and then follow the money. Moreover, look to tradition and use your common sense. Is there a cultural tradition somewhere in the world that confirms this trend? It's hard to go wrong with traditional foods like fruits, vegetables, grains, beans, nuts, and seeds.

FRUIT LEATHER

Fruit leather from pulp is not as sweet as typical fruit leather, so feel free to sweeten this recipe with sweetener such as Stevia or coconut nectar to suit your taste. You may use any mixture of sweet fruit for this recipe, including apples, pears, oranges, or strawberries.

Yield: 2 Leathers

1 cup fruit juice	Stevia or other sweetener
1¹/₂ cup fruit pulp	to taste (optional)

1. In a large mixing bowl, combine the fruit juice and fruit pulp. Stir in the Stevia.

2. Place a layer of plastic wrap or parchment paper over 2 dehydrator trays, unless you have a tray made specifically for leathers, and spoon half the mixture onto each tray. Spread the mixture onto each tray with a spatula until it is about ¹/₄-inch thick at the sides, ¹/₈-inch thick at the center, and 9-¹/₂ inches in diameter.

3. Dehydrate the mixture at 135°F for 6 hours, or until it is leathery and has no wet spots. Once the leathers are done, roll them up in the plastic wrap and store them in the refrigerator. If you used parchment paper, roll them up in the paper and place them in a plastic bag.

For a Change . . .

Add spices, chopped nuts, or coconut to make this recipe your own. If you want to keep it raw, dehydrate at 105°F for about 12 hours.

THE POWER
OF POPSICLES

Frozen pops are a great way to sneak veggies into your family's diet while also using any excess seasonal produce you may have on hand. When made with fresh juice, they are a treat you can give to your kids without an ounce of guilt. For kids who are used to processed foods, it is probably best to start with frozen pops made exclusively of fruit juice and pulp. You could use bottled juice in combination with some fresh pulp, but when frozen pops are made with freshly extracted juice and pulp they become powerhouses of nutrition.

You can use a fair amount of vegetable pulp and juice in a frozen pop and still have it taste like a treat. For finicky eaters, you may want to increase the amount of fruit pulp and decrease the amount of veggie pulp. The only thing needed to make these treats is a popsicle mold. The following instructions are based on my mold, which makes ten 3-ounce pops, and apply to all the recipes offered.

1. Blend the ingredients in a blender until smooth.

2. Carefully pour the mixture into a popsicle mold, leaving ¼-inch space at the top of each popsicle to allow it to expand as it freezes.

3. Place the popsicle mold in the freezer for approximately 5 hours, or until the popsicles are solid.

4. Unmold the popsicles by dipping the mold in warm water until the popsicles are loose enough to remove.

I have also included a few recipes for pops here, but feel free to use your own creativity when making frozen treats and look upon this information simply as a guide.

Frozen Raspberry Pops
2 cups apple juice
1/2 cup raspberry juice (approximately 12 ounces raspberries)
2 tablespoons beet juice
1/2 cup beet pulp
Stevia or other natural sweetener to taste (optional)

Frozen Lemon-Lime Pops
1 cup cucumber juice
1 1/2 cups green grape or apple juice
2 tablespoons lemon juice (1/2 lemon juiced with the peel)
2 tablespoons lime juice
1/2 cup cucumber pulp
Stevia or other natural sweetener to taste (optional)

Frozen Dream Pops
1 2/3 cup orange juice
1/2 cup carrot juice
1/2 cup carrot pulp
1/3 cup coconut cream
1 teaspoon vanilla extract
1-inch piece tangerine peel (optional)

Helpful Tips

• Carefully pour the mixture into the mold, wiping around the top of the mold with a towel to make sure it stays clean and dry.

• If you try to unmold the pops too quickly they will fall apart. Thankfully, they may be quickly placed back into the mold and frozen until solid without a problem.

• Pineapple juice and pulp hide vegetable pulp particularly well.

• Make rainbow pops by pouring different colors of blended juice and pulp into the same mold without mixing.

• Try different flavors like ginger, mint, a bit of turmeric root, or herbal tea mixed with fruit juice for truly gourmet pops.

BEET CAKE

Cakes made with whole grain flour are sometimes heavy, but this one has a marvelously spongy and moist texture. The flavor is great too.

Yield: 12 Servings

2 cups whole grain spelt flour

2 teaspoons baking powder

$1/4$ teaspoon baking soda

1 teaspoon allspice

1 cup raisins

$1/2$ cup beet pulp

$1/4$ cup coconut oil

12.3-ounce package extra firm silken tofu

$1/2$ cup maple syrup or coconut nectar

$1/2$ cup beet juice

1 tablespoon apple cider vinegar

1 teaspoon vanilla extract

1. Preheat the oven to 350°F. Grease a 9-inch square cake pan with coconut oil and sprinkle it with flour. Set aside.

2. In a large mixing bowl, sift together the spelt flour, baking powder, baking soda, and allspice. Add the raisins and beet pulp. Mix well to distribute evenly, using your hands if necessary.

3. In a blender, combine the coconut oil, tofu, maple syrup, beet juice, apple cider vinegar, and vanilla extract. Blend until smooth and creamy.

4. Add the wet ingredients to the dry ingredients. Using a spatula, mix just enough to combine the two.

5. Pour the batter into the prepared baking pan and bake for 40 minutes, or until a toothpick inserted in the center comes out clean. Allow the cake to cool in the pan for 5 minutes before slicing, or transfer it to a serving plate and allow it to cool.

For a Change . . .

You can easily make a tasty pink icing for this cake by combining 3 to 4 tablespoons beet juice, 1 cup cream cheese (I always opt for a nondairy version), and $2/3$ cup fruit-sweetened raspberry jam in a blender and blending until smooth.

BEET BROWNIES

I find most brownie recipes unpleasantly sweet, so I created one that is scrumptious without being cloying. This gluten-free brownie hides a good deal of beet pulp within its dark chocolate deliciousness. With almost every ingredient measuring $1/2$ cup, these instructions should be very easy to follow.

Yield: 16 Brownies

$1/2$ cup mashed medium silken tofu

$1/2$ cup beet juice, nondairy milk, or water

$1/2$ cup maple syrup or coconut syrup

$1/2$ cup coconut oil

1 teaspoon vanilla extract

$1/2$ cup garbanzo flour

$1/2$ cup cocoa powder

$11/2$ teaspoons baking powder

$1/2$ cup beet pulp

$1/2$ cup chocolate chips

$1/2$ cup chopped nuts or chocolate nibs

1. Preheat the oven to 350°F. Grease a 9-inch square cake pan with coconut oil and sprinkle it with flour. Set aside.

2. In a blender, combine the tofu, beet juice, maple syrup, coconut oil, and vanilla extract. Blend until smooth and creamy.

3. In a large mixing bowl, sift together the garbanzo flour, cocoa powder, and baking powder. Mix well. Add the beet pulp and mix well, making sure to distribute it evenly throughout the dry ingredients. Stir in the chocolate chips and nuts.

4. Add the wet ingredients to the dry ingredients. Mix well until batter forms.

5. Pour the batter into the prepared baking pan and bake for about 25 minutes, or until a toothpick inserted in the center comes out clean. Allow the brownies to cool in the pan for 15 to 20 minutes before slicing them into 16 squares of equal size.

CARROT CAKE WITH ICING

My stepdaughter loved this cake when I made it for her dad's birthday. It is very good without the icing, but spreading a nice layer of the icing on top of the cake certainly makes it extra special.

Yield: 12 Servings

2 cups spelt or whole wheat pastry flour

2 teaspoons baking powder

$1/2$ teaspoon baking soda

1 teaspoon cinnamon

$1/2$ teaspoon nutmeg

$1/4$ teaspoon ground cloves

$1/2$ cup carrot pulp

$1/2$ cup raisins

$1/2$ cup walnuts or pecans

12.3-ounce package extra firm silken tofu

$1/2$ cup carrot juice

$1/2$ cup maple syrup or coconut nectar

$1/4$ cup coconut oil

1 tablespoon apple cider vinegar

ICING

1 cup soft pitted dates

$1/2$ cup carrot juice

2 tablespoons coconut oil

$1/2$ cup cashew butter or raw cashews

1 teaspoon vanilla extract

1. Preheat the oven to 350°F. Grease a 9-inch square cake pan with coconut oil and sprinkle it with flour. Set aside.

2. To prepare the icing, combine the dates, carrot juice, coconut oil, cashew butter, and vanilla extract in a blender. Blend until very smooth, using a spatula to scrape the sides of the blender as needed. Set aside.

3. In a large mixing bowl, combine the flour, baking powder, baking soda, cinnamon, nutmeg, and ground cloves. Mix well. Add the carrot pulp and raisins. Mix well to distribute them evenly, using your hands if necessary. Set aside.

4. In a blender, combine the tofu, carrot juice, maple syrup, coconut oil, and apple cider vinegar. Blend until smooth and creamy.

5. Add the wet ingredients to the dry ingredients. Using a spatula, mix just enough to combine the two.

6. Pour the batter into the prepared baking pan and bake for 40 minutes, or until a toothpick inserted in the center comes out clean. Allow the cake to cool in the pan for 5 minutes, or transfer it to a serving plate and allow it to cool. Ice the cake.

CARROT DATE SQUARES

This is an easy way to turn carrot pulp into a delectable treat. Delicious does not have to mean complicated or unhealthy.

Yield: 8 Squares

1 cup carrot pulp	1 tablespoon coconut butter
$1/2$ cup soft pitted dates	$1/2$ teaspoon cardamom
$1/2$ cup almonds	2 tablespoons chopped pistachios or unsweetened shredded coconut, divided
$1/2$ cup cashews	

1. In a food processor, combine the carrot pulp, dates, almonds, cashews, coconut butter, and cardamom. Grind until the mixture holds together.

2. Sprinkle 1 tablespoon chopped pistachios on the bottom of an $8^{1}/_{2}$-x-$4^{1}/_{2}$-inch loaf pan. Spoon the mixture into the pan, distributing it evenly. Press firmly so that the mixture holds together. Sprinkle the remaining 1 tablespoon chopped pistachios over the mixture and press firmly again. Cover and store in the refrigerator for 1 hour before slicing into 8 squares of equal size.

For a Change . . .

Instead of using a loaf pan, you can spoon the mixture evenly into 8 small dessert cups and top each with chopped pistachios. This alternative take will taste a lot like the Indian sweet confection known as carrot halwa.

NUTRITIOUS YOU CARROT CAKE

This no-bake cake is as pretty as it is delicious, and it uses a lot of pulp. It's easy to make but contains a number of steps, so make sure you try this one when you have enough time to dedicate to it.

Yield: 12 Servings

$1^1/_2$ cups rolled oats

1 cup pecan halves

1 cup dried cranberries

1 cup pitted dates, soaked for 20 minutes and then drained

4 cups carrot pulp

$1/_2$ cup coconut butter, melted

$1/_2$ cup shredded coconut

3 tablespoons melted coconut oil,

1 teaspoon cinnamon

$1/_2$ teaspoon candied ginger

1 teaspoon vanilla extract

$1/_4$ teaspoon salt

ICING

3 cups cashews, soaked for 2 hours and then drained

2 tablespoons lemon juice

3 tablespoons coconut oil

$1/_4$ cup maple syrup

$1^1/_2$ cup water

$1/_2$ teaspoon vanilla extract

$1/_8$ teaspoon salt

1. Place the rolled oats in a Vitamix or food processor. Process until finely ground. Transfer to a large mixing bowl.

2. Place the pecans in the Vitamix or food processor. Process until coarsely ground. Transfer to the large mixing bowl.

3. Place the dried cranberries in the Vitamix or food processor. Process until coarsely ground. Transfer to the large mixing bowl.

4. Place the dates in the Vitamix or food processor. Process into a paste. Transfer to the large mixing bowl.

5. Add the carrot pulp, coconut butter, shredded coconut, coconut oil, cinnamon, candied ginger, vanilla extract, and salt to the large mixing bowl. Mix well, using your hands if necessary.

6. To prepare the icing, combine the cashews, lemon juice, coconut oil, maple syrup, water, vanilla extract, and salt in a Vitamix or food processor. Process until very smooth and creamy.

7. In an 8-inch springform pan, place half the cake batter. Transfer to the freezer for about 2 hours, or until solid.

8. Remove the cake from the freezer and ice it with half the icing. Return the cake to the freezer for about 4 hours, or until the icing is solid.

9. Repeat step 8. Remove the cake from the freezer and refrigerate until thawed. If you remove the cake from the freezer in the morning, it may be served in the evening. The unfrozen cake may be stored in the refrigerator for 3 to 5 days.

The Difference is Huge

Once you begin eating more healthfully, you may have to retrain your taste buds. If you are used to eating processed foods, which are high in sugar, salt, and fat, it may take a while to learn to love the taste of fresh, nutritious food, but before long you will again be able to recognize the wonderful natural sweetness of fruit and the delicious variety of flavors found in vegetables. You will also wonder how you were ever able to enjoy all that old junk, which will taste far too sweet and artificial to your refreshed palate.

BEET SWEETS

Open your mind and prepare your taste buds for this extraordinary snack. The cardamom, allspice, and ground cloves make these sweets a truly special treat.

Yield: 12 Balls

1¹/₂ cup cashew pieces	¹/₂ cup raisins
¹/₄ cup flax seeds	¹/₂ teaspoon allspice
¹/₂ cup beet pulp	¹/₄ teaspoon cardamom
¹/₄ cup coconut sugar	Pinch of ground cloves

1. Place the cashews in a blender. Grind them into a fine powder.

2. Place ground cashews in a medium-sized mixing bowl, reserving ¹/₄ cup in a small mixing bowl.

3. Place the flax seeds in the blender. Grind them into a fine powder. Add the ground flax seeds to the medium-sized mixing bowl with the cashews. Add the beet pulp, coconut sugar, raisins, allspice, cardamom, and ground cloves. Mix well, using your hands.

4. Shape the mixture into 12 walnut-sized balls. Roll each ball in the reserved ¹/₄ cup ground cashews and place them all in a covered container in the refrigerator. Chill the balls for 2 hours before serving.

Helpful Tip

Unless you have a very powerful blender, the cashews may have to be ground in two batches.

CHOCOLATE AND PEANUT BUTTER BALLS

I promise you will be amazed by how good these balls are. I also promise no one will know they are full of pulp! This recipe is especially easy to accomplish with a Vitamix, but a food processor will work, too. You will simply have to work a little harder to grind the ingredients fully.

Yield: 26 Balls

1 cup carrot pulp

1/2 cup unsweetened shredded coconut or ground peanuts

1 cup soft pitted medjool dates

3/4 cup crunchy peanut butter

1/2 cup cocoa powder

1. Place the carrot pulp in a large mixing bowl. Set aside.

2. Place the shredded coconut in a small mixing bowl. Set aside.

3. In a Vitamix or food processor, combine the dates and peanut butter. Process until relatively smooth, using the plunger of the Vitamix or a spatula to scrape the sides of the machine as needed.

4. Add the mixture to the large mixing bowl. Add the cocoa powder and knead well.

5. Shape the mixture into 26 balls of equal size. Roll each ball in the cocoa powder and coconut mixture and serve immediately, or store in a covered container in the refrigerator.

For a Change . . .

Use almond butter and 1/2 teaspoon almond extract instead of peanut butter, and roll the balls in ground almonds.

THE SECRETS OF SORBETS

Most ice cream and sorbet machines make about 1 quart frozen dessert. All you need to create fresh juice and pulp sorbets is about 4 cups juice and pulp mixture. Freezing usually takes only 20 minutes. Almost any fresh fruit juice can be turned into sorbet, and most of the time all the pulp, or at least a good deal of it, can be incorporated, too. If you don't have an ice cream and sorbet maker, it is still pretty easy to make sorbet by freezing the juice and pulp mixture in ice cube trays and then processing the frozen cubes in a food processor or Vitamix. Whether you make sorbet in an ice cream maker or ice cube trays, be sure not to make it too far in advance of eating, as it will freeze solid and need to be broken up and blended again. Nevertheless, you can make sorbet up to 4 hours before serving, storing it in a covered container in the freezer and stirring it every hour.

Using pulp in sorbet changes its consistency, so if you are making this dish for children or elderly people, who may prefer a smoother sorbet, add less pulp and more juice. I can't think of any fruit that shouldn't be used to make this delicious treat. The better the fruit, though, the better the sorbet, so do your best to use produce that is in season. Depending on the sweetness of the fruit, you may wish to add sweetener, and my preference here would be Stevia. If you don't like Stevia, however, any sweetener you choose should do the trick.

Most fresh fruits do not need added flavors to make wonderful sorbet, but the right touch can make take a recipe from delicious to wow! A few ideas for additions include essential oils (food-grade only) such as peppermint, cinnamon, or lavender; teas such as lemongrass, green tea, or chamomile; and floral waters such as rose water or orange flower water. Of course, in the case of essential oils of herbs or other plants, you may instead juice these herbs or plants and use their fresh juices to the same effect.

PEAR-MINT SORBET

Healthy and luscious when made with ripe pears, this sorbet is an elegant end to a dinner party. Serve it with raspberries and mint leaves for a little extra pizzazz.

Yield: 1 Quart

$2^1/_2$ cup pear juice   10 drops Stevia, or to taste

$1^1/_2$ cup pear pulp   Extra mint leaves as garnish

1 cup fresh mint leaves, juiced

1. In a large mixing bowl, combine the pear juice, pear pulp, mint leaf juice, and Stevia. Mix well.

2. Transfer the mixture to an ice cream maker and process until frozen, or transfer the mixture to ice cube trays, freeze, and then remove the cubes from the trays and blend them in a food processor until desired consistency is reached. Garnish sorbet with the extra mint leaves and serve immediately.

Helpful Tip

This sorbet can be stored for 3 to 4 hours in a covered container in the freezer. Just be sure to stir it once every hour before serving. If you need to store it longer, place it in a shallow covered container. To serve after more than 4 hours in storage, break up the frozen mixture with a knife and blend it in a food processor or Vitamix.

Pretty Smart

Freeze apple-lemon juice, cucumber-fennel juice, apple-cranberry juice, watermelon juice, or any other fruit juice in ice cube trays. Use these cubes to chill and add flavor to water, punch, or herbal tea.

BLACK GRAPE
AND ROSE WATER SORBET

While I find black grapes quite special, any type of grape will do in this recipe. I enjoy the texture of grape skin in this sorbet, but feel free to blend it with the black grape juice until it is no longer pulpy if you'd prefer a smoother sorbet.

Yield: 1 Quart

$2^1/_3$ cup black grape juice	**$^1/_2$ cup black grape pulp**
1 cup apple juice	1 tablespoon rose water

1. In a large mixing bowl, combine the black grape juice, apple juice, black grape pulp, and rose water. Mix well.

2. Transfer the mixture to an ice cream maker and process until frozen, or transfer the mixture to ice cube trays, freeze, and then remove the cubes from the trays and blend them in a food processor until desired consistency is reached. Serve immediately.

Helpful Tip

This sorbet can be stored for 2 to 3 hours in a covered container in the freezer. Just be sure to stir it once every hour before serving. If you need to store it longer, place it in a shallow covered container. To serve after more than 4 hours in storage, break up the frozen mixture with a knife and blend it in a food processor or Vitamix.

A Five Dollar Shake

Add fruit or vegetable pulp to a shake or smoothie along with the other ingredients. Just remember that pulp is drier than whole produce, so you will need to add enough liquid to achieve a nice consistency, and enough fruit to make it yummy.

Metric Conversion Tables

COMMON LIQUID CONVERSIONS

Measurement	=	Milliliters
1/4 teaspoon	=	1.25 milliliters
1/2 teaspoon	=	2.50 milliliters
3/4 teaspoon	=	3.75 milliliters
1 teaspoon	=	5.00 milliliters
1 1/4 teaspoons	=	6.25 milliliters
1 1/2 teaspoons	=	7.50 milliliters
1 3/4 teaspoons	=	8.75 milliliters
2 teaspoons	=	10.0 milliliters
1 tablespoon	=	15.0 milliliters
2 tablespoons	=	30.0 milliliters
Measurement	**=**	**Milliliters**
1/4 cup	=	0.06 liters
1/2 cup	=	0.12 liters
3/4 cup	=	0.18 liters
1 cup	=	0.24 liters
1 1/4 cups	=	0.30 liters
1 1/2 cups	=	0.36 liters
2 cups	=	0.48 liters
2 1/2 cups	=	0.60 liters
3 cups	=	0.72 liters
3 1/2 cups	=	0.84 liters
4 cups	=	0.96 liters
4 1/2 cups	=	1.08 liters
5 cups	=	1.20 liters
5 1/2 cups	=	1.32 liters

CONVERTING FAHRENHEIT TO CELSIUS

Fahrenheit	=	Celsius
200–205	=	95
220–225	=	105
245–250	=	120
275	=	135
300–305	=	150
325–330	=	165
345–350	=	175
370–375	=	190
400–405	=	205
425–430	=	220
445–450	=	230
470–475	=	245
500	=	260

CONVERSION FORMULAS

LIQUID		
When You Know	Multiply By	To Determine
teaspoons	5.0	milliliters
tablespoons	15.0	milliliters
fluid ounces	30.0	milliliters
cups	0.24	liters
pints	0.47	liters
quarts	0.95	liters
WEIGHT		
When You Know	Multiply By	To Determine
ounces	28.0	grams
pounds	0.45	kilograms

About the Author

Vicki Chelf is an experienced natural foods cooking instructor, accomplished artist, and internationally recognized food writer. She has written and coauthored numerous cookbooks, including *The Arrowhead Mills Cookbook, Cooking for Life*, and *Vicki's Vegan Kitchen*. For over thirty years, she has taught groups and individuals how to prepare plant-based dishes. She believes that anyone can become a good cook, and that cooking delicious and nutritious fresh food is easy with a little guidance. For more information, additional recipes, and kitchen wisdom, or to share your own pulp recipes, visit Vicki's blog at www.pulpkitchen.org.

Index

LIVE FOODS LIVE BODIES!
Recipes for Life
Jay and Linda Kordich

Through years of healthful living, Jay and Linda Kordich have learned that abundant energy, enhanced mental clarity, and a sense of contentment and well-being are easily within reach. In *Live Foods Live Bodies!*, they reveal all their secrets, including juice therapy and a living foods diet. This powerful book—lavishly illustrated with beautiful full-color photos—was designed to help you transform the person you are into the person you want to become.

The book is divided into three parts. Part One begins with the inspiring story of Jay's recovery from cancer through healing juices and reveals the power of live foods. Part Two guides your transition to a living foods diet and details what's needed in a health-promoting kitchen, from tools and appliances to fresh foods. Part Three presents well over one hundred kitchen-tested recipes for delectable salads and dressings, breakfasts, juices and nut milks, soups, spreads, and much more. No matter how old you are, Jay and Linda will show you that you can live healthier and happier with *Live Foods Live Bodies!*

$18.95 US • 240 pages • 7.5 x 9-inch quality paperback • ISBN 978-0-7570-0385-1

JUICE ALIVE, SECOND EDITION
The Ultimate Guide to Juicing Remedies
Steven Bailey, ND, and Larry Trivieri, Jr.

The world of fresh juices offers a powerhouse of antioxidants, vitamins, minerals, and enzymes. The trick is knowing which juices can best serve your needs. In this easy-to-use guide, health experts Dr. Steven Bailey and Larry Trivieri, Jr. tell you everything you need to know to maximize the benefits and tastes of juice.

The book begins with a look at the history of juicing. It then examines the many components that make fresh juice truly good for you— good for weight loss and so much more. Next, it offers practical advice about the types of juices available, as well as buying and storing tips for produce. The second half of the book begins with an important chart that matches up common ailments with the most appropriate juices, followed by over 100 delicious juice recipes. Let *Juice Alive* introduce you to a world bursting with the incomparable tastes and benefits of fresh juice.

$14.95 US • 288 pages • 6 x 9-inch quality paperback • ISBN 978-0-7570-0266-3

VICKI'S VEGAN KITCHEN
Eating with Sanity, Compassion & Taste
Vicki Chelf

Welcome to *Vicki's Vegan Kitchen*! Come on in. There's always room for anyone who wants to experience the pleasures of vegan cooking. After all, it's no secret that dishes made with fresh local ingredients that are properly prepared are absolutely delicious . . . and the healthiest that the planet has to offer. As Dr. T. Colin Campbell's comprehensive China Study has shown, there is an undeniable link between a vegan diet and the prevention of serious health conditions, including heart disease, cancer, type II diabetes, and autoimmune diseases. And as you are about to discover, *Vicki's Vegan Kitchen* is the perfect cookbook to support this healthy dietary lifestyle. In it, author Vicki Chelf—cooking teacher and decades-long follower of the vegan diet—shows you just how easy it is to prepare divinely delicious plant-based foods.

The book begins with an overview of the vegan diet, including its nutritional benefits and impact on weight control. Chapters on kitchen staples, cooking methods, and food preparation techniques come next, along with helpful guidelines on shopping for the best-quality foods and ingredients. Over 375 of Vicki's favorite recipes and recipe variations follow. She shares delectable breakfast choices—from pancakes and waffles to hot cereals and scrambles—and shows you how to make to make heavenly breads, perfect pie crusts, and incredible homemade pasta (you won't believe how easy it is). You'll even learn how to make your own "moo-less" milks! Vicki also provides her collection of luscious dips and spreads, sensational soups and salads, and satisfying bean dishes, as well as pilafs and other grain creations, veggie favorites, a collection of scrumptious desserts, and so much more. To help ensure successful results, step-by-step directions accompany each recipe, and instructional drawings appear throughout. Every dish is a winner—easy to make, completely vegan, and utterly delicious.

Once you step into *Vicki's Vegan Kitchen*, you won't want to leave. Along with enjoying the delicious, satisfying food it offers, you will ultimately enjoy the radiant health that it brings.

$17.95 US • 320 pages • 7.5 x 9-inch quality paperback • ISBN 978-0-7570-0251-9

THE WORLD GOES RAW COOKBOOK
An International Collection of Raw Vegetarian Recipes
Lisa Mann

People everywhere know that meals prepared without heat can taste great and improve their overall health. Yet raw cuisine cookbooks have always offered little variety—until now. In *The World Goes Raw Cookbook*, raw food chef Lisa Mann provides a fresh approach to (un)cooking with recipes that have an international twist.

After discussing the healthfulness of a raw food diet, *The World Goes Raw Cookbook* tells you how to stock your kitchen with the tools and ingredients that make it easy to prepare raw meals. What follows are six recipe chapters, each focused on a different ethnic cuisine, including Italian, Mexican, Middle Eastern, Asian, Caribbean, and South American dishes. Whether you are already interested in raw food or are exploring it for the first time, the recipes in this book can add variety to your life while helping you feel healthy and energized.

$16.95 US • 176 pages • 7.5 x 9-inch quality paperback • 978-0-7570-0320-2

EAT SMART, EAT RAW
Creative Vegetarian Recipes for a Healthier Life
Kate Wood

As the popularity of raw vegetarian cuisine continues to soar, so does the evidence that uncooked food is amazingly good for you. From lowering cholesterol to eliminating excess weight, the health benefits of this diet are too important to ignore. Now there is another reason to go raw—taste! In *Eat Smart, Eat Raw,* cook and health writer Kate Wood not only explains how to get started, but also provides kitchen-tested recipes guaranteed to delight even the fussiest of eaters.

Eat Smart, Eat Raw begins by discussing the basics of cooking without heat. This is followed by twelve chapters offering 150 recipes for truly exceptional dishes, including hearty breakfasts, savory soups, satisfying entrées, and luscious desserts. There's even a chapter on the "almost raw." Whether you are an ardent vegetarian or just someone in search of a great meal, *Eat Smart, Eat Raw* may forever change the way you look at an oven.

$15.95 US • 184 pages • 7.5 x 9-inch quality paperback • ISBN 978-0-7570-0261-8